PREPPED AND READY

*The Ultimate Guide To Prep   or
Future Hazards A*

Introducing the PREPPERS 7 STEP PLAN
TO KEEPING SAFER DURING
FUTURE PANDEMICS and DISASTERS

(Essential Kit Lists, Tips, Advice and Survival Hacks)

BY

DAVID "Dingo" PUGH

© Copyright 2020 by David Pugh

All rights reserved.

This document is geared towards providing exact and reliable information with regards to the topic and issue covered. The eBook is sold with the idea that the publisher is not required to render accounting, officially permitted, or otherwise, qualified services. If advice is necessary, legal or professional, a practiced individual in the profession should be ordered.

From a Declaration of Principles which was accepted and approved equally by a Committee of the American Bar Association and a Committee of Publishers and Associations.

In no way is it legal to reproduce, duplicate, or transmit any part of this document in either electronic means or in printed format. Recording of this eBook is strictly prohibited and any storage of this document is not allowed unless with written permission from the publisher. All rights reserved.

The information provided herein is stated to be truthful and consistent, in that any liability, in terms of inattention or otherwise, by any usage or abuse of any policies, processes, or directions contained within is the solitary and utter responsibility of the recipient reader. Under no circumstances will any legal responsibility or blame be held against the publisher for any reparation, damages, or monetary loss due to the information herein, either directly or indirectly.

Respective authors own all copyrights not held by the publisher.

The information herein is offered for informational purposes solely, and is universal as so. The presentation of the information is without contract or any type of guarantee assurance.

The trademarks that are used are without any consent, and the eBook of the trademark is without permission or backing by the trademark owner. All trademarks and brands within this book are for clarifying purposes only and are the owned by the owners themselves, not affiliated with this document.

PREPPERS 7 STEP PLAN

KEEP SAFE DURING
PANDEMICS and DISASTERS
(Essential Kit Lists, Tips, Advice and Survival Hacks)

How to better Survive future pandemics, COVID-19 may be getting under control, but sadly, do not think that future pandemics will not happen again; this was far from the first pandemic in the world. In 1918, a third of the world's population got infected with "Spanish Flu" resulting in an estimated 50 Million deaths https://www.cdc.gov/flu/pandemic-resources/basics/past-pandemics.html

Why else should you be more prepared? famines and crop failures, natural disasters, economic and financial collapse, fuel shortages, EMP Strike (electromagnetic pulse which kills all electronics), *war and terrorism type events.*

Whilst no scholarly expert, at age 57 and with a lifetime of experience in bushcraft and general preparedness, I do feel somewhat qualified to pass on these key crucial lessons which I have learned whilst on my prepper journey.... but the learning is ever ongoing like life lessons are....

FOLLOW ME *for all the latest info and prepping updates*
BLOG: www.PreppedAndReady.co.uk
TWITTER: **David Pugh MAFS Prepper**
INSTAGRAM: **mafs_prepper**
INFO SITE: www.Dingo-Preppers.co.uk

IN THIS BOOK
- **Learn the 7 key steps needed to become better prepared and crisis ready**
- **Learn how to defend and protect your family, loved ones, and your possessions**

- This is a simple, easy to follow 7 Key-Step Plan for better preparedness
- This plan is suitable and designed for all men and women *(18+ is advised because of some of the content of prepping)*
- Get the most comprehensive UK based kit lists for Everyday Carry Bags (EDC bags), Bug Out Bags, and also Get Home Bags

This book consists of 3 levels of preparedness. You get to choose how far you wish to take your preparedness journey, whatever works best to fit in with you and your family's lifestyle.

For ease of demonstrating this, a Traffic Light system is used for each of the 7 key steps covered within this book.

GREEN: This section is for people to go and "START" on their Prepper journey
These are the biggest and most vital fundamental steps in being "Prepped and Ready."

AMBER: Stay in **GREEN** or work up to next level preparedness.
The "PROFICIENT" level.
These Amber tasks and learnings will take you slightly more out of your comfort zone,
as you learn how to be even better prepared in readiness for more serious situations.

RED: Stay in AMBER or work up to next level preparedness.
Keen to even further develop your skills? "ADVANCED" level is true Prepper territory.
Don't stop now...You love this stuff and are all in with your prepper lifestyle and skills

CHAPTERS
1. Introduction
2. My background
3. 7 Key Step Plan and getting started....
    GREEN pages *Starter level*
    AMBER pages *Proficient level*
    RED pages   *Advanced level*
4.   STEP 1: Food and Water Stockpile Supplies
5.   STEP 2: Buy and create your own "Everyday Carry Bag" (EDC)
6.   STEP 3: Home based security and home defences
7.   STEP 4: Comprehensive Medical supplies list
            CPR and First Aid Introduction
8.   STEP 5: "Bug Out Bag" and "Get Home Bag"
9.   STEP 6: Shelter building, Fire starting, and Bug Out survival.
            Constructing simple snares and traps to catch food
            Preserving food you have caught/trapped.
            Wild Foods and Foraging basics.
            Essential Knot tying
            More advanced water collection techniques

10. STEP 7: Krav Maga and Self Defence training
11. **CONCLUSION,** summary and further advancement studies
12. **INDEX: -**
    INDEX 1: Knife law in the UK
    INDEX 2: Bibliography of books I have enjoyed and found useful. All in some part have aided me in creating this Prepper book
    INDEX 3: Thanks and acknowledgments

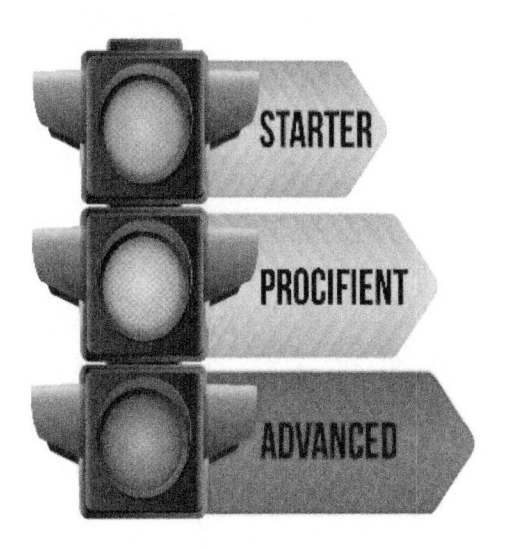

Chapter 1
Introduction..10
Chapter 2
My background..15
Chapter 3
The 7 Step Traffic Light Plan.......................................24
Chapter 4
STEP 1
Food and Water stockpiles..27
UK Food Supply Chain FACTS....................................28
Prepper Long-Life Foods and storage.......................33
Barter Goods TOP 10 list..37
Chapter 5
STEP 2
Everyday Carry Bag (EDC) and Kit List......................42
Chapter 6
STEP 3
Home Security and Home Defence..........................48
Chapter 7
STEP 4
Medical Supplies Kit List and First Aid......................57
Boots and blisters...63
Tourniquets, Wounds and Broken Bones................64
HYPO and HYPER-thermia, Frostbite and CPR........67
Chapter 8
STEP 5
Bug Out Bag and Kit List..70
Get Home Bag and Kit List...86
Chapter 9
STEP 6
Woodland Shelter Building..91
Fire Starting..98
Dakota Fire Pit..103
Swedish Log Fires...105
Rocket Log Fire Stoves...108
How to Trap and Snare Animals..............................109
How to Butcher your prey.......................................121
How to Preserve your caught food.........................126

Canning techniques..130
Root Vegetable Cellars...134
PEMMICAN the "ultimate survival food"..138
Wild Foods and Foraging...139
Essential Rope Knots...143
Advanced Water Collection Techniques..145
Chapter 10
STEP 7
Krav Maga Self-Defence..149
Chapter 11
Conclusion, Summary and further advancement...........................152
Chapter 12
INDEX 1: UK Knife Law..153
INDEX 2: Bibliography of books..156
INDEX 3: Acknowledgment and thanks..167

CHAPTER 1

INTRODUCTION

Prepping or Survivalism *is a movement of individuals or groups (called survivalists or preppers) who actively prepare for all manner of emergencies, be it natural or man-made. Including possible disruptions in the social or political order, on scales from local to international.*

The "typical" prepper can often be seen wearing an iconic looking gas mask. But in reality, most preppers are fairly regular everyday people, just ones who are way more prepared though than the average person....
If COVID-19 in 2020 has taught us anything, it is that we all need a little more preparation in our lives.

Thousands, even just hundreds of years ago, our ancestors would not have been able to go to their local supermarket and buy whatever supplies they needed. This idea of a weekly shop, in historical terms, is a very new concept. Previously, even our great grandparents better understood the need to store and preserve their food, knowing that it was necessary to sustain them through long periods and during harsh winters, etc.
In today's society, people take this ever supply of food and essentials for granted and assume that a shop will always be open and stocked up to give them anything they need…. I believe a lot of people had quite a shock during COVID-19 when foods, medical equipment, and toilet paper got scarce and rationed. There is a greater awareness and appreciation of the benefits of becoming better prepared should another pandemic or disaster occur, which is why I am writing this book.

The intention of this book is not to create fear in you. In fact, it is quite the opposite. By taking action, you will feel far more empowered and in control of your life and that of your family.
If you want to learn more about some preppers fears and predictions regarding future disasters, I suggest you search online for these topics…. they

are a pretty scary read, though. More pandemics / Super Volcanoes (6 of these around our Earth) / Solar Flares / Global Warming / Future Nuclear Wars and Civil unrest / Subterranean Gas Deposits / Financial Collapse / Asteroid impact / Storms and Flooding, Hurricanes, Tornados and Tsunamis / even the prospect of Artificial Intelligence being a cause for an apocalyptical even (*Perhaps Arnie had something there with SkyNet afterall*)

WHY DID I START PREPPING?
You will have your own reasons and backstory for wanting to learn how to be better prepared in your life and able to cope with whatever life may send your way!

For me, over the years, as various events occurred in my life, I took positive steps to be better prepared should such situations ever occur again…. That, to me, basically sums up who a prepper is.

Being prepared is a mind-set and a way of life. I have an everyday carry bag (EDC) but will provide more information about this bag and its contents later. This bag comes with me in most places, either at the bottom of a rucksack or in the boot of my car. It has, over the years, being added to and improved. I now believe it is the most comprehensive EDC bag possible for my personal preferences. Really great for such a small bag as it comes full of really useful essential and helpful kit... I even have a "His N Hers" version, so my partners get protected and prepared too!

Preppers like myself no longer seem quite so crazy after the 2020 pandemic hit the world, with little or no warning. I believe that after the COVID-19 pandemic, far more people will choose to become just a little bit better prepared in their lives should another event occur. The UK lost in the region of 50,000 lives, but frankly, if things had been a little different, these numbers could have been just the tip of the iceberg. We have all seen world news and scientific opinions on how much worse the situation could have been. This is far from scaremongering; these are documented and difficult facts from scientists around the world.

As of October 2020, here are the rounded up, worldwide stats on the COVID-19 pandemic, and this is the world getting off lightly...
Cases – 34 Million
Recovered - 25 Million
Deaths – 1 Million

Being a prepper meant I had my food stockpiles and yes, even toilet paper stocks! In fact, I did not have to go to the supermarket for five weeks. So, while everyone else was panic buying, I, on the other hand, was able to give my family, friends, and others, access to food supplies and even the wonderful gift of toilet paper, hand sanitiser, and protective face masks. Consequently, I was not a burden on the scarce supplies available to our local communities in those vital early weeks of panic buying or putting myself at risk by going out into the community.

I even had 200 of the N195 face masks and a lot of hand sanitisers that were bought when these things were still cheap to buy and readily available; family and friends were pleased with that, for sure. You will never catch a prepper "panic buying" with the masses.

However, on a more positive note, the fact that you are reading these words means you have taken the first, and most importantly, the biggest step in wanting to take steps to be better prepared should future events occur. Hence, welcome to these **7 key steps plan** and keep your family and loved ones safer and far better prepared for unexpected events in life.

In this book, I cover all the essential basics in helping you become better prepared for disasters. Most prepper books originate from the USA, where prepping is very much "next level" and often focuses a lot on guns and ammunition. I wanted to create a more "mainstream" prepper book for everyday men and women, specifically for the UK and Europe. Here, gun laws are very different, and available land far more scarce. In the USA, it is also very easy to lose yourself in their vast wilderness, enabling people to far easier hide out until things calm down.

The focus for writing this prepper book is fairly unique; it is written to be suitable for most men and women to incorporate some level of prepping into themselves and their family's everyday lives.

Essentially, this book concentrates on "stay at home" prepping and disaster survival. This, in the main, this means having access to sufficient food, water, medical supplies, and other essentials readily stockpiled available for you, your pets, and your loved ones in case of any unexpected disaster, whether that be another pandemic, worldwide crop failures, food or fuel shortages, etc.

Upon completion of this 7 key step plan, you will discover you now possess the mindset and confidence that, if required, you will know you are ready and better prepared to safeguard your home, family, and possessions. I promise you that if you follow and complete this 7 key step plan, you will feel far more fully in control of your life. Knowing that you are more self-reliant and far less dependent on others is actually a very empowering feeling indeed....

For more advanced prepper development, it is useful to consider bug out bags and locations, advanced food storage preps, etc. A bug out location is, simply put a "safe" evacuation location that you know of and are familiar with. For example, a secluded woodland, ideally one you own, otherwise, a place you know is which is quiet and in a fairly secluded location. Here, you will be able to prepare ready cache storage of all your family's essential survival supplies. Usually buried in watertight containers that only you and your family know the hidden location for. Be careful if you do not own the land; burying supplies in someone else's land is obviously not a legal practise! Consequently, most people in modern life have their supplies ready packed to go, kept in a nearby storage unit or their home garage/sheds, or even at their place of work.... Still close to hand for being ready to "bug out" at short notice.

But this is for more advanced preppers, which I do briefly cover in this book. But for now, let's work together and first get you home prepped and better ready to face whatever may come your way.

> **TIP**: Mums the word, become more like our British Elite Special Air Service, special forces (SAS), become The Grey Man... i.e., Don't stand out, stay under the radar, and do not brag or openly discuss your preps and food caches. Until the publication of this book and a TV show of which I was part of, the majority of my family and friends had no idea I was even a prepper!

CHAPTER 2

What's My Background?

I'm just a regular guy, reasonably fit for my age, but I'm not an athlete, and I'm not ex-special forces, that's for sure.
But what I am is a family man who loves his family and will do anything to protect and keep them safe. I do not like to rely on anyone else, nor do I need to because I am prepared and in possession of a strong survival mindset. I am capable and confident in my prepper abilities, and after completion of this 7 key step plan, I believe you will too.

My friends know me as "Dingo Dave," a nickname I earned in 1985 during a year spent hitchhiking and travelling through Australia. A chance encounter with a wild dingo (Australian wild dog) in the outback near Alice Springs probably started my "being prepared" or Prepper journey. I was hiking in a very remote location, and no one knew where I was, nor would I have quickly been looked for or found had I never returned. Mobile phones or even the internet was not even a thing back in those days (yes, I am that old)

Being an avid animal lover, especially with a fondness towards dogs, while eating some of my packed lunch, I spotted a dingo cautiously eyeing my food. Dingo's, to my mind, look like emancipated German Shepherds (Alsatian dogs), so feeling a bit sorry for this sad-looking "dog" in such a hot, arid red dust landscape made me decide to share some of my lunch. After throwing him some ham from my sandwich, he decided it tasted far better than his usual fare of rabbit or roadkill and thus emboldened, he made a play for the rest of my lunch. As I discovered, Dingo's have surprisingly big and numerous teeth for such small looking dogs!
A short scuffle and a little bloodletting, mainly on my side, even today 35yrs on, there remain a faint trace of a scar on my hand from our wild encounter. Symbolically, in my mind, because this is exactly how I see city life quickly becoming should our civilised society falter, and our population suddenly run

out of food. People will soon turn into crazed rabid animals when faced with no way of feeding themselves or their families!

The moral of the story, I guess, was my unconscious beginning to become more like a Boy Scout, with a "Be Prepared" mindset, something that remains part of my core values to this very day.
Consequently, after this incident, I travelled with a couple of extra things, so I was more "prepared" a knife (*I know not very politically correct in today's climate, but knives, when sensibly used, are a key and vital prepper tool/emergency method for self-defence*), in addition, I carried a small first aid kit and a torch…. the beginnings of my first Everyday Carry Bag (EDC), not that the bag even had a name back then!

When I reflect back over a life well lived involving lots of traveling and adventures, I have experienced many dramatic encounters, each one of these slowly transitioning me further and further along my Prepper lifestyle journey. I was never actually conscious of even being a prepper until about 3 years ago. While watching some of the Netflix television series such as Doomsday Preppers, Doomsday Bunkers, American Preppers, Southern Survival, etc., I realised that I had evolved into a true Prepper, and I found that my hobby actually had a name for it as well. I discovered I was indeed a "Prepper," and actually, I was far from being the only one with this mindset too.

Just to give some relevance to my prepper choices, here are some key moments in my life that, over time, that transformed this average Joe into a true prepper…
- The wild dingo-dog meeting already mentioned
- I once saw a car crash directly in front of me, and it rolled onto its roof. The doors were crushed shut, and I had to kick the rear windscreen to get the occupants out. It is surprisingly difficult to kick in a windscreen whilst wearing trainers. So from that day forward, I always try to keep a glass breaker and seat belt cutter, be it in my car or in my EDC Bag (everyday carry bag). Nowadays, it has become a

common device that many people carry in the cars or attach to their car keyring.
- My teenage son once got attacked by a group of youths and got slashed with a knife; he needed stitches and now has a visible scar near his eye as a daily reminder of this nasty incident. After this, I did a lot of research into the best and most effective form of self-defence. I ended up selecting Krav Maga, an Israeli special forces fighting system. It was great fun training with my son, Ironically, he was the youngest in the class, and I was the oldest. Interestingly, I subsequently discovered that Krav Maga is the fighting and self-defence system most widely endorsed by prepping groups. I believe that is because It is very much a "real life" hands-on fighting system. Not so much "Self Defence" as "Defence and Counter Attack".
- Three years later, five armed attackers invaded my home; the instincts from training Krav Maga kicked in, and on autopilot and "muscle memory" from my training drills, I managed to put up enough of a fight that they eventually fled empty-handed. Had I not been prepared with my training, things would definitely have ended up very differently.
- I once came across someone who was having a heart attack, thankfully the emergency services were really great and talked me through what to do, and the ambulance quickly arrived. However, I was left feeling that had I not being able to so easily call the emergency services for assistance, maybe whilst out hiking somewhere remote with no mobile phone reception, etc., that I was ill-equipped to offer effective lifesaving aid. Consequently, a week later, I booked to attend a Medic First Aid and CPR (Cardio Pulmonary Resuscitation) Course. So should something like this ever happen again, I will be better equipped to give effective assistance. That's why my EDC bag (everyday carry bag) now even has a CPR face mask in it. (These masks make giving the "kiss of life" safer for you in case there's blood, vomit, etc. all over the victim's face, or like during COVID-19, when you would not offer breathes, especially without a protective mask). Learning at least some basic first aid is essential for everyone.

- I have seen accidents occur during mountain hiking, and this has led me to carry emergency aluminium space blankets, first aid kits, etc. so that I can offer some level of at least basic help. There have been many times when my stash of plasters, antiseptic cream, paracetamol, and especially anti-diarrhoea tablets have been very gratefully received by fellow hikers in some level of urgent help. Being prepared is NOT about only facing huge disasters; it is all about being better equipped to deal with whatever life may throw at you, be that large or small.
- A couple of severe winters ago, my car got stuck in deep snow. The breakdown services could not reach me until the following day. Having a "prepared" mentality meant during winter, my car always had an emergency box of blankets, water, food and snacks, emergency strobe lights, a fully charged mobile phone power bank, etc. All of which made my night stranded in my car far more bearable. Following this chilly night spent stranded in my car overnight, I now also carry snow chains. Prepping is a lifestyle, and you will keep learning and evolving based on what life sends your way. Being a prepper means constant learning and improving your prepper readiness based on your life and the everyday events in it.

"If you fail to prepare, then prepare to fail" this is one of my favourite phrases.

Here in the UK, prepping is a fairly quiet, almost underground activity. As mentioned, for me, virtually no family or any of my friends was even aware that I was a prepper. Not from any form of secrecy, it just never came up in conversation. They all knew I enjoyed bushcraft and that I was always a really organised person, I was largely the go-to guy if you were stuck or had a problem you needed help with.... this could be as simple as helping out with car battery jump leads, tyre inflator, etc. It's not like my house was full to the brim with food stores on shelves here, there and everywhere, with all rooms piled high with supplies. My 3+ months' worth of tinned foods, pasta, rice, and other essentials (yes, including toilet rolls) were either in my prepper shed or under all of our beds (All my beds have those hydraulic struts enabling you to store stuff under the bed…. you would be very surprised by how many tins of food can fit under a standard double bed.)

As already mentioned, the UK prepper community is VERY DIFFERENT from the more featured USA market. Preppers in America concentrate a lot more on weapon stockpiles, and they are far more extreme in their preps than preppers in here the UK. Weapons are largely illegal in the UK and most of Europe, so weapons are not a major UK prepper requirement…we make do with knives, axes, and even crossbows, these being the most popular UK defensive weaponry choices. In addition, they are more than adequate to see off most aggressors if you have the correct mindset and can show aggressors that you are trained, able, and indeed very willing to defend what's yours. The majority of potential attackers will avoid you when they realise you are not such an easy target after all; they will soon head off in search of easier targets. For example, most burglars will choose a house without an alarm or pet dog to break into, over one with CCTV, alarms, and dogs, because these houses are obviously far better prepared to deal with a potential robbery and consequently, more difficult and far riskier to break into.

My EDC bag (everyday carry bag), a small bag about 6" wide and 9" tall, is often in the boot of my car, or at the bottom of my rucksack when out hiking, even if with a reduced kit contents list, inside my suitcase when off on holiday. It is not permanently over my shoulder…. Just somewhere unobtrusive but usually always fairly close to hand. It is not that I avoid talking about prepping, but I am fully aware that to most other people, preppers are seen as the crazy weirdos who stockpile food, equipment, weapons, water, fuels, etc. Perhaps, after the 2020 COVID-19 pandemic, preppers will be viewed in a slightly more positive light now, and our numbers increase as more people get into being better prepared…. Imagine if everyone in had even just one month's food and key supplies at home, then panic buying, inflated supermarket, and medical prices would have been unnecessary. But I'm obviously talking to the converts here. Simply because you have bought this book and are actually reading these words, you have already decided that you want to become far better prepared and better able to face whatever the future may send your way.

Being prepared, in my opinion, is sanity, not craziness. I like to know that I can, to some degree, be largely self-reliant in keeping myself and my loved ones fed, watered, and protected thanks to my supplies and my preparedness. I have always enjoyed being able to look after myself and others, and not to rely entirely on anyone or anything else; it's quite a confidence-building and liberating feeling. This even carries over into my dream home; I would love one day to live "off-grid," creating my own power, having my own water source, heating, drainage, sewage, etc. A small farm with livestock and vegetable crops would be the icing on the cake for me in becoming truly "self-sufficient" ...So far, I've only managed chickens for eggs and solar panels for some free off-grid electricity. There is still a long way to go. Sadly, society does not let us easily achieve this dream. In the UK, we have some of the strictest planning regulations on where and how people can choose to live their lives. Society is more geared toward consumerism and conformity, sadly. That said I am now in the process of buying a secluded woodland, one with its own fresh water spring.

Apart from the self-sufficiency angle, prepping gives me a quiet confidence that whatever life and the world can throw my way, at least food and essentials will not be an issue in short to a medium timeframe for me. Prepping can be expensive; after all, it's not cheap to stockpile 3-6 months' worth of food and supplies. You will know what your own monthly food budget is, well now multiply that by 3 or 6, that's your rough budget in set up costs. However, think of it as savings, food costs seem to keep increasing. Therefore, whenever supermarkets have great special buy offers on, that's my time to bulk buy and stockpile supplies. Then think like a supermarket and rotate your food stores to always ensure your prepper stock has the very longest use by dates, i.e., Store the shortest foods by "use by dates" at the shelf front, then use these foods as part of your regular food consumption and replace with new. Your food preps are no different than having a great big food pantry, just bigger and able to sustain you for far longer.

Here's another example of your preps being a form of savings, during the 2020 COVID-19 pandemic, my Airbnb income property went from high income for me to zero almost overnight, then in the same week, I was made redundant from my job of 10 years. Like so many families in the UK and indeed worldwide during this pandemic, our incomes dropped off a cliff, and serious belt-tightening was essential.... now, let's think how a prepper can dramatically economise in such dire times? We just started to consume our stockpiles of food and supplies. Awesome, because apart from buying some fresh veg, no supermarket bills for the foreseeable future for me...see prepping can be viewed as just another form of savings or insurance policy. Sounds a bit cleverer and more logical now, doesn't it?

Prepping is obviously not for everyone; it may be better to just think about "being prepared." However, many people do feel it's a bit extreme and a little bit weird, and in many people's opinion, fairly unnecessary. They are content in largely leaving their security, their wellbeing, and their very survival in the hands of the government, the police, and the emergency services......great when it works and whilst society conforms. Thankfully it did during the COVID-19 crisis.... But it could easily have been very different had the virus spread far faster, and the effects of contracting the virus had been worse.

Remember the effects of Hurricane KATRINA in New Orleans 2005 and the horrific events in the weeks before the government could get aid and order restored. *(https://en.wikipedia.org/wiki/Hurricane_Katrina)*. It makes for sobering reading, overall, most people act honourably and with kindness towards each other, but sadly there will always be the gangs, the bullies, the immoral, the rapes, robberies, looting, destruction, and even murder. It is quite frightening just how fast humanity can actually fall apart.... Think back to your school days reading the book "Lord of the Flies" *(Lord of the Flies is a 1954 novel by Nobel Prize-winning British author William Golding. The book focuses on a group of British boys stranded on an uninhabited island and their disastrous attempt to govern themselves)*

For me, prepping is not the overriding belief or thought of some imminent doomsday event occurring that originally got me interested in beginning prepping. I was actually expecting events such as transport strikes meaning foods and supplies not reaching the supermarkets causing food shortages; I never dreamt that something like a virus could hit the world so hard and cause such chaos so frighteningly fast. For me, my prepping pastime has during this COVID-19 pandemic proved somewhat of a lifesaver, both mentally and financially, in my being able to live off the food stockpile and having plenty of key pandemic essentials such as the facemasks, hand sanitisers, and even toilet-rolls. My prepping took away from me most of the anxiety and stress, which I know most other people had to face. Thankfully, our government did get our food and supply chains very quickly back on track quickly but had it taken longer, who knows how quickly civil unrest and looting, etc. could have occurred.

Most supermarkets have very little storage capacity, so the majority of their food and produce is out on the shelves. If the lorries stopped bringing the food re-supplies, most supermarkets would run out within 24 hours!!!!! So having some of your own food supplies stockpiled makes perfect sense…. But more on this later, with some sobering published facts and statistics.

Let's now start to get YOU better prepared…
By the fact that you are here and reading through this book, you are obviously looking to put things in place to ensure your family and loved ones are far better prepared and protected should another event occur. Unfortunately, another event is quite likely…be it another superbug, a natural disaster, fuel or transport strikes stopping food reaching the supermarkets, civil unrest, and rioting or any manner of things from small scale events to ones more seismic in scale.

What follows now is all the basic information you need to better protect your family by following these 7 key steps. The 7 steps are modular, meaning that you can choose to carry out all or just some of them. How far you choose to take your prepping is a hugely personal decision….it will be very dependent upon your own life and the reasons behind what made you decide to buy this book.

If you choose to remain a starter prepper or choose to go onto become more proficient or even reach advanced preparedness...that is your choice, and this will be your journey. I hope you enjoy it; I sincerely believe that whatever level you choose, it will make you more mentally strong, more confident, far more in control of your life and destiny, and with less anxieties about events that are otherwise outside of your control.

However, I guarantee that if you follow through and complete all or even just the beginner level of these 7 key step plans that you will sleep better at night knowing that you are in a far more secure position should, God forbid, disaster strikes again.

Good luck, you can do this, you have it....

CHAPTER 3

So what is this 7 Key Step Plan?

This book plan consists of 3 levels of preparedness.
You can choose how far you wish to take your preparedness journey, what works best to suit your lifestyle and your family.
To demonstrate this, I use a Traffic Light system for this 7 key step plan.

GREEN pages. This section is for people to go "START" their Prepper journey
These are the biggest and most vital fundamental steps in Being better "Prepped and Ready."

AMBER pages. Stay in **GREEN** or work up to the next level preparedness. The "PROFICIENT" level.
These Amber tasks and learnings will take you slightly more out of your comfort zone, as you learn how to be even better prepared in readiness for more serious situations.

RED pages.   Stay in AMBER or work up to the next level preparedness. Keen to even further develop your skills? "ADVANCED" level is true Prepper territory.
Don't stop now…You love this stuff and are all in with your prepper lifestyle and skills

The Key 7 Steps which we will cover are: -
1. **Food, water, and key supplies**
2. **Everyday Carry Bag (EDC Bag)**
3. Home based security and home defences
4. Medical supplies and first aid training
5. Bug Out Bag and bugging out evacuation locations.
6. Shelter, fire building, wild foods, advanced and survival techniques
7. Krav Maga and self-defence training

Getting started

This 7 key step plan involves getting you fully focused and having the right mindset to succeed.

These will test you in every aspect of your life and your personality. They will push you practically, physically, mentally, and even financially *(i.e., your chosen level of commitment with the purchase of food/water/medical supplies: More information and spending guides on this later)*. There's way more to prepping than just a big shop down at your local supermarket.

It Starts NOW.... *"If you fail to prepare, prepare to fail"*
"If you never start, then you can never finish" – LIFE
"By changing nothing, nothing changes." – TONY ROBBINS, Author and motivational speaker

What this book costs you will be the easiest and the cheapest part of this entire prepping process.

Accept that in purchasing food, water, and medical stockpiles, etc., plus optional self-defence training WILL COST YOU. Think of this expenditure as an investment in yourself, your family, and your loved ones. 99% of your expenditure is not lost money, its visible money in the form of actual supplies you have bought, or new skills you have acquired! You have not fritted it away, quite the contrary.... you are investing in your health, your wellbeing, and in extreme circumstances, perhaps even in the survival of your family. Plus, you will be mentally a far more alert and aware person. Not forgetting the fact that if you keep up the fitness self-defence training, you will also be a far healthier and fitter version of the present you.

Your purchase of food/water/medical/toilet rolls/toothpaste etc. can obviously be built up slowly over time. Some preppers begin by just spending an extra 10% at the supermarket on each week's food purchases in order to buy extra food and supplies and put into their prepper supplies. Or, my favourite option, bulk buy whenever supermarkets hold a great low-priced promotion offer, such as discounts or buy one get one free type offers. These are great and easily achievable methods to begin building up your survival stockpiles.

However, you may want to get going and build your food stockpiles far faster, so if this is your preference, I suggest you register at a big cash and carry outlet such as our UK brands such as BOOKER, MAKRO, or COSTCO, etc. These are usually trade only outlets, but most of us know someone with their own business who can help us get registered to have a trading card from these outlets. Then simply pay cash or on your own credit card...simple.
If you do prefer to buy everything fast and easily in bulk, that's why these trade outlets are your best "fast track" option to getting all your supplies in as little as just one day.

BOOKER   https://www.booker.co.uk/home.aspx
MAKRO   https://www.makro.co.uk/in-store-shopping.html
COSTCO   https://www.costco.co.uk/
+GOOGLE   Cash and Carry outlets in (add your location)

You are now about to begin this 7 step programme, and it will change your life.

CHAPTER 4

The Start Of The 7 Step Plan

Step 1: Food and Water Stockpile Supplies

> **TOP TIP and KEY POINT:** To stock up on an absolute minimum of one to three months of food and supplies. One month's food and essential items will help you get through most "minor" events. Think back to when COVID-19 first hit the UK; the first 2-6 weeks were when food, hand sanitiser, face masks, thermometers, and yes, even toilet rolls were most in short supply. By just having even a month's supplies in your home will help avoid many of the panic buying anxieties experienced by most other people.
>
> In this Book, we are concentrating on home-based preps, such as what would have been really useful prior to the 2020 COVID-19 crisis. Extra foods and essential supplies would have proved super useful, and for many people, it would also have greatly reduced their anxiety and stress levels

Imagine if our Prime Minister here in the United Kingdom, Mr. Boris Johnson, had NOT recovered from the COVID-19 virus and had become another one of our sad death toll statistics. Now imagine a possible scenario in which our government faltered even just for a short time, maybe delaying key decisions on solving food shortages or citizen's protective measures did not get actioned quite fast enough.... with severe food shortages, it's estimated that rioting and serious public disorder could occur within 2 to 3 weeks!

First, here are some sobering FACTS from **WHICH Magazine**: JULY 2020 publication www.which.co.uk
Which magazine published some very interesting facts following the COVID-19 pandemic. I directly quote from their July 2020 magazine issue....

"The COVID-19 factor... The fragility of our food supply chains was laid bare when COVID-19 hit the UK, and nervous shoppers combined with a relatively small demand for extra food had a huge effect.
At first, the underlying supply hadn't changed – the problem was getting stock to customers fast enough.
All food logistics and retail employees were classed as key workers. Initial worries about absentee rates due to self-isolation didn't seriously materialise, thanks in part to huge recruitment drives.
Supermarkets tried to meet demand by limiting product ranges, rationing, and restricting opening hours to allow time to restock.
But empty shelves were just one consequence of the COVID-19 outbreak.
While retail sales soared, food-service demand plummeted as restaurants and cafes closed.
The solution seems obvious: take the food destined for restaurants and sell it in shops. But it hasn't been that simple. Milk produced for coffee shops has been poured down the drain and steaks earmarked for restaurants flogged at knock-down prices."

I strongly suggest you try to become an online member to read the full article; it is a worrying read! Also, WHICH has lots of other benefits from being a member, it is well worth joining.

If the COVID-19 pandemic had been more severe, food supplies would run out very quickly.
The below image, taken again from the above **WHICH** article, shows just how much of our foods depend on imports. We export very little, so if global

supply chains dry up or even slow down slightly, the shortage in the UK will be felt quickly.

The Solution?
Very simple, now that our supermarkets are back up to speed and there are no current shortages, **NOW is the time to start building up your food and water stockpiles**. Remember, even as little as one whole month's storage of food/water and essentials will have a big impact. Imagine if the majority of citizens had just this extra month of food stocks, it would have virtually eliminated the need for mass panic buying and anxieties about worrying if/how you will be able to feed your family....

The image below shows UK food import/exports (as per The **WHICH Magazine**: JULY 2020 publication)
This clearly shows the huge imbalance and reliance for the entire UK on imported foods.... Ask yourself what would happen if flights stopped, no more ships docked, and no overseas food delivery trucks arrived....

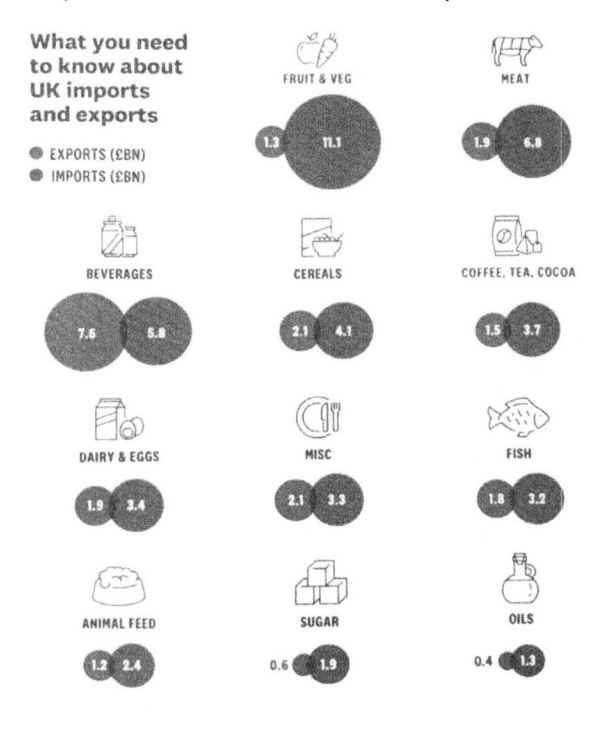

What you need to know about UK imports and exports
- EXPORTS (£BN)
- IMPORTS (£BN)

Category	Exports	Imports
FRUIT & VEG	1.3	11.1
MEAT	1.9	6.8
BEVERAGES	7.6	5.8
CEREALS	2.1	4.1
COFFEE, TEA, COCOA	1.5	3.7
DAIRY & EGGS	1.9	3.4
MISC	2.1	3.3
FISH	1.8	3.2
ANIMAL FEED	1.2	2.4
SUGAR	0.6	1.9
OILS	0.4	1.3

Hopefully, these facts have convinced you that this book is NOT intended to scare people, but rather to provide you with options and information about the actual fragility of the key essentials in our lives that we rely on and actually take for granted. It is like your health; you do not appreciate it till it's gone!

Next, let's look at home-based food cache preparations.
The general rule of thumb is 1/3/6 or even 12 months of supplies stockpiled.

Your final decision on storage levels will often come down to a few key factors: -
1. The level of self-sufficiency you personally prefer having. A level at which you feel comfortable with having to hand
2. Finance: If food shopping for a month costs you say GB £400, then a 3-month supply will cost about GB £1,200 in investment. Therefore, finances will affect the prepper's planning.
3. Local or worldwide news/events, putting you on a high or low level of an alert to possible danger. For instance, the worldwide COVID-19 pandemic hit quite fast with only a few months warning even to those with a keen ear for potential news threats. If you were better attuned to possible dangers, you would have time to stock up even more supplies while supermarkets are still fully functioning, and there are no shortages. Thinking ahead, you could predict things escalating and take early action way ahead of time.

Personally, I like the 3- 6-month food stockpile levels. I believe it is sufficient for most short-term events. During this COVID-19 pandemic, the first 3 months had the biggest impact on supermarket shortages, sudden panic buying, and general population unrest, and heightened anxiety before the government managed to get a handle on things. That said, I now intend moving up to a 9 to 12-month stockpile, possibly half home based and half at my secret woodland bug out location for added safety.
Even me, an avid prepper, am only just entering the advanced mindset stages. More about bug-out locations in Step 5.

The more extreme preppers go all out and invest in expensive army type rations, which can have a shelf life of up to 20+ years. Here in the UK, the majority of preppers take a slightly less doomsday approach. For me, I prefer to be eating the same type of foods that I currently eat. So I tend to buy mainly dried and tinned foods which have an already long shelf life; these are usually* safe to eat long after the best before dates *(*BUT caution. Your safety is your priority; eating foods past best-before dates may involve risk to your health. I am not suggesting you use food past its expiry date)* so long as the tins are intact with no signs of damage, rusting or swelling, etc. they do tend to still be totally safe to eat (more on this later).

So for me, I stock up on all my usual favourites, and I rotate these emergency food stores with my regular foods, thereby always rotating the supplies and ensuring the longest best before dates remain in my food stores. Think of your prepper stores simply as your extended food pantry.

I'm a bit of a list guy, maybe a bit OCD too (*Obsessive Compulsive Disorder*), ok...definitely OCD to be honest, but who doesn't like a good checklist?
I advise you to keep a record of what you buy each week or each month from your supermarket shop; this will aid you in knowing what items to buy and in what sort of quantities. Or simply buy extras on top of your usual shop and put those extras straight into your prepper supplies. Obviously, you need to ignore fresh veg, etc. and supplement those portions with their equivalent as tinned veg, it is important that you stock what is right for you and your family and what you all enjoy eating as much as possible, keeping in mind any special dietary needs.

Common sense is vital too, not only in your food selections but also in using food from your stores. For instance, if food when opened, smells, or looks "off" then do not risk eating it. Store your canned tins in a cool, dry location, do not store any damaged, dented tins, etc., avoid moisture as this will damage the tins and cause them to start rusting. In a serious situation which has led you to need to utilise your preps, then you do not want to risk becoming ill.... You must be in a position to be able to physically protect your family, home, and your supplies. Plus, in very worst-case scenarios, doctors and hospitals may not even be an option to go to anymore for help.

Of special note and consideration must be: -
- Does anyone in your family have allergies or special dietary needs?
- Anyone vegetarian, vegan, etc?
- Does anyone need food supplements?
- Foods for infants, plus nappies, creams, etc.
- Foods for your pets.
- Which foods have the best protein or nutrients?
- Which foods last the longest? For instance, white rice will last almost indefinitely if correctly stored in moisture-proof air sealed containers, whereas brown rice, which has a high oil content, can go bad in just months.
- As a general rule, foods with a high oil or high moisture content will only last a long time if they're dried, canned, or otherwise preserved. Out of interest, honey is immortal and lasts forever! Jars of honey discovered in Egyptian pyramids are still safe to eat today. It may darken and even form sugar crystals, but that's harmless and still totally safe to eat. Making honey storage as a sweetener an ideal staple for your prepper supplies.

Here are a few common prepper tips on long-life foods and storage

WARNING: Using foods that are past their "Best Before Date" has to be an individual's personal decision and cannot be 100% safely endorsed as best or safe practice.
SEE https://www.youtube.com/watch?v=iYTbhqOBWJA

DRIED PASTA: (NOT the type made using eggs though. Type made from semolina, flour, and water are best) This can be kept almost indefinitely!
TEA: can easily be useable 6-12 months after its "best by" date
POWDERED MILK: can easily be useable 12 - 18 months after its "best by" date.
BEEF JERKY: can easily be useable 12- 24 months after its "best by" date.
TINNED/CANS: can easily be useable 2-5 years after its "best by" date. So long as the tins have not been subjected to intense heat, avoid dented cans and those with "swollen" tops, which could indicate bacteria build up inside.
STOCK CUBES: Little bouillon cubes like OXO used for stock or soups, if kept dry and well-sealed, can easily be useable many years longer than its "best by" date, although the taste will degrade over time
BAKING POWDER: A longer life as an alternative to yeast for bread making.
PEANUT BUTTER: If unopened jar, it can easily be useable 24 months plus after its "best by" date. After a couple of years, you may notice the oil separating and some loss of flavour. But will easily last far longer than 2 years after its "best by" date.

DARK CHOCOLATE: Because milk chocolate contains more diary, best store dark chocolate with a high cacao content and little or no milk. If stored in a cool place, it can easily be useable 5 years after its "best by" date. If white spots appear, this often means it got too hot. However, it is still safe to eat.

LIQUOR: Hard liquor and spirits can last almost indefinitely due to its high alcohol content. It is also considered as a preppers favourite "barter" item.

WHITE RICE: (*not long-grain variety due to high oil content*) White, Wild, Arborio, Jasmine, and Basmati Rice are the best types of rice to store indefinite shelf life if stored correctly (Avoid Brown rice, due to high oil content it only lasts a few months) However, take note, if tiny black bugs appear (weevils, common in ruining rice and flour). If these have got in, it's ruined. So important to store in thoroughly dried airtight containers. But occasionally, they still appear as it's possible their eggs got harvested with the rice itself, rare, but possible.

TIP: I have heard if you freeze it when you first buy it, that this will kill off any weevils or eggs.

EGGS: Rub fresh eggs all over with olive oil (stops air getting in), and they will stay fresh for up to a year unrefrigerated (turn the eggs monthly to stop the heavier yokes falling to the bottom and sticking to the shell). Powdered dried eggs are another good food store.

SALMON/TUNA, tinned: Shelf life is anything up to six years, and these offer very high amounts of quality protein and essential healthy fats.

VEGETABLE OIL: Best cooking oil to store due to its long shelf life compared with lard etc.

MEATS, tinned: Corned beef, SPAM, Chicken, Tinned Pies, etc.

Meals Ready to Eat (MRE): Meals Ready to Eat are popular with Preppers, Survival, and Bushcrafters. An MRE is simply a Meal Ready to Eat, most people think of military meals, but there are any numbers of civilian versions on the market. Good quality but can be expensive. More suited to "Bug Out" bag use as often light and easy to carry, compared to putting a dozen tins of canned food in your rucksac...But not necessary here for our HOME based preps and food stores.

DRIED BEANS and PULSES: If kept dry, these are pretty much indestructible. After about two years, they will lose much of their moisture and will require pre-soaking and often need longer cooking times to become edible again. Another long life, high protein food that is easy to store, though. They can be used to mix with all other foods, offering you a bulkier and more filling meal. Dried beans provide an excellent source of high fibre nutrition, including protein, as well as a source of iron, magnesium, and zinc.

Aduki beans / Black beans/ Black eyed peas/ Butter beans/ Cannelloni beans/ Edamame (soy beans) buy only organic or you will risk having GMO beans/ Fava beans/ Garbanzo beans/ Green beans/ Kidney beans - ideal for chilli/ Lima beans/ Lentils/ Navy beans / Pinto beans - staple for chilli/ Red beans/ White beans.

Just so you are aware, here are few basic introductions to just some of the more advanced food storage methods.

Advanced Food Storage and Canning (*canning is not necessarily tin cans, it's more often the process to boil food in glass jars and sealing with lids. Canning removes oxygen and destroys any enzymes, and prevents the growth of bacteria/mold. Factors that cause fresh food to spoil*). Also, consider learning how to make your own jams, preserves, pickles, and even dehydrating foods.

There are also more advanced ways of calculating food store requirements, but frankly, at this "starter" stage, I would recommend just buying more of your usual food types and not worry too much about advanced techniques. That said, it is always good to have some general knowledge of other ways of calculating your food stores!

Here's one which is based on **calorific values,** for example.
For instance, here is a rough daily food calorie requirement for males to consume:
Boys   9-13yrs Moderate activity 1,800-2,000 / Active lifestyle 2,000 - 2,600

Boys 14-18yrs Moderate activity 2,400-2,800 / Active lifestyle 3,000+
Men 19-30yrs Moderate activity 2,600-2,800 / Active lifestyle 3,000+
Men 31-50yrs Moderate activity 2,400-2,600 / Active lifestyle 2,800 - 3,000
Men 51yrs+ Moderate activity 2,200-2,400 / Active lifestyle 2,400 - 2,800

Another popular advanced method is the **proportional** food store method…
IE.
15% PROTEINS: Meats, Peanut butter, assorted nuts, etc.
35% GRAINS: Cereals, pasta, rice, bread making
20% VEGETABLES: Corn, carrots, peas, etc. (Tinned is easiest for long life)
15% DAIRY: Powdered milk, hard cheese, etc.
15% FRUITS: Canned and dehydrated fruits

While I think it important for you to be aware of such advanced methods, details, and thoughts…. please do not stick to that at this stage. Your home food storage preps are, in a basic sense, just long shelf life versions of what you already eat on a regular basis. For example, canned carrots instead of fresh carrots, so your meal plans I suggest, should not be too different from your everyday lifestyle foods, based on your own and your family's preferences and tastes.

Anyway, back to our home-based food storage considerations; my personal formula follows the basic calculations below about the amount of dry coffee is needed for my personal 3-month prep supplies: -
I drink at least 8 cups of strong black coffee daily, no milk, no sugar
My favourite jar of coffee is a 300g jar.
I use a heaped spoon, so I spooned out a whole jar of coffee and discovered I get 130 spoonsful per jar.
130 divided by my average consumption of 8 cups a day = 16.25 days of coffee per jar.
3 months = average 91 days, divided this by the 16.25 per jar of coffee
So, the maths works out that I need 6 x 300g jars of coffee for my 3-month food cache.

Had I drank my coffee with milk and sugar, then I would need to do the same calculations for the milk and sugar also, based on powdered milk, though not your usual fresh milk.
I get through an average of 2 tins of baked beans a week, so typically over 3-month that equates to needing 24 can of baked beans.

So my planned 3 months' food shopping list started with: -
6 x Jars of coffee
24 x Tins of Baked Beans
3 x 5kg packs white rice
(*a 5kg bag works out sufficient to give you a serving of rice every day for one month, per person*)

So the calculations are pretty simple and straightforward. The easiest way to start is to record everything that you (and your family) eat in a week, then work out the portion sizes, and you will soon have a pretty accurate shopping list to start you off.

Barter Goods

Personally, I'm a little dubious about the benefits of stockpiling "barter" items, especially for someone in a "starter" home-based stage of prepping. However, always good to have an awareness of some of these more advanced prepper concepts.
I like the principle, but in reality, if people find out you have these prime key products, you might become an even bigger target.

> **TIP:** NEVER trade weapons; today's friend could well become tomorrow's enemy!

Here's a list though of the top 10 most popular Prepper barter items, as well as the obvious food and water. The good news is that most of these items will already be in your food stores. It might just be worthwhile to stock up on even more of these key items, just in case: -
1. Alcohol
2. Tobacco and Cigarettes

3. Salt (also a great preserver)
4. Sugar / Honey
5. Coffee / Tea
6. Medical Supplies
7. Heirloom Seeds, for growing fresh veg and produce
8. Toiletries (toothpaste, soap, condoms, feminine products, washable baby nappies, etc.)
9. Toilet Paper
10. Chocolate (Stays edible even if gone white with sugar crystals forming)

Water Storage

Just buy bottled water in sealed containers and store them in a cool, dark place. Commercially sealed water bottles, stored properly, will remain fresh virtually forever! When in doubt, it can simply be boiled before drinking anyway.

Personally, I like the 5-gallon water office cooler type bottles. You can even fit these with easy to use hand pumps to dispense directly from containers when needed.

As a rule of thumb, it is calculated that for water, an adult will require *approx.* 1 gallon / 4.5 litres of water every day, and that's with them being super careful in using it.

Thus one 5 gallon / 22½ Litre container of water will last approximately a week.

Based on this, you will need 4 x 5-gallon containers <u>per person</u> for <u>every month</u> as an absolute minimum of drinking water you store.
(not forgetting your pets needs and some for washing, etc.)
If you have access to a water source, such as a nearby stream, river, or just from rainwater collection, you can boil the water to make it safe for drinking. Otherwise, add water purification tablets to it.
(More about this is our advance water storage/collection section later)

TIPS:
- Do NOT reuse containers that have previously stored milk or fruit juice. It is virtually impossible to clean them well enough for storing water on a long-term basis.
- As your water supply needs to cover personal hygiene such as washing, teeth cleaning etc. It is advisable to add a good stock of moist wipes to your prepper stores and use these for a lot of your personal hygiene needs instead of using up your valuable water stores.
- Store your valuable water away from any cleaning agents, chemicals, or fuel, to avoid any possibility of contaminants coming into contact with any of your water.
- CONDOMS – non-lubricated condoms are a great addition to your prepper bags. Not only for the obvious benefits but they are strong enough to actually hold up to 2lts of water, or become an improvised glove to protect a hand or finger injury and even a perfect container to protect and keep precious fire tinder dry!
- Set up rainwater collection at your home, maybe even a series of connected water butts. Water is valuable, and rainwater can be boiled or filtered for drinking or used for washing clothes/dishes, etc. You can store a lot of water at home quite simply this way and in a very unobtrusive way. A ceramic water filter is an ideal purchase as it uses gravity to work, so no external heat or power is required. I personally use a countertop Doulton Gravity Water Filter System, only

50cms H x 26cms diameter. Another popular brand to look at is the Berkey Gravity Water Filter System.

> **TIP:** *This is a useful non-emergency water filter, as it will remove the Fluoride and any other water treatment chemicals such as Ammonia from your regular household tap water, making it taste so much nicer.... Although the Fluoride is there to protect your teeth.*

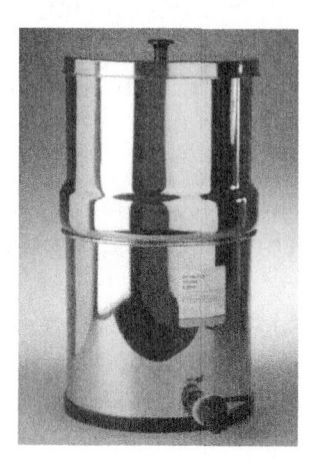

As in this book, we are looking at home-based prepping or "Bugging In" as it is often referred to, for your food/water storage needs.

Another great bit of kit is a **WaterBOB**. Basically, it is a huge water bladder you put in your bath tub. The idea is to fill it up if you believe the water supply to your home may get turned off. Even a regular problem, for example, notice given by your water company that they need to do scheduled repairs and your water will be off for a period of time. This bladder will hold 100 gallons/450 Litres of water, enough for an average family of 4 to carefully live on for almost a month!

41

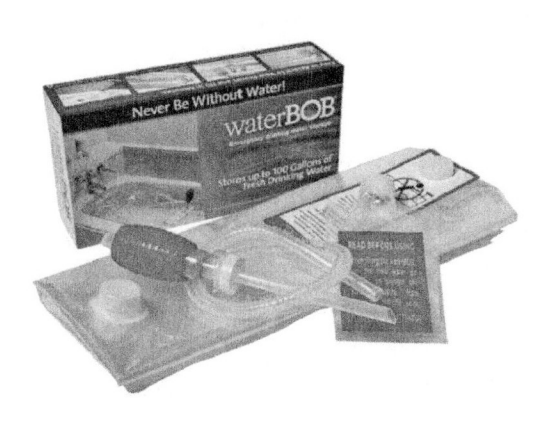

CHAPTER 5

STEP 2: Buy And Create Your Own Everyday Carry Bag (EDC)

> *TOP TIP and KEY POINT: Begin by looking very carefully at my personal of 3 different EDC bags contents list, then create your own bag or bags. Also, start getting used to carrying this with you, or having it in your car, in your rucksac whilst out hiking, etc.*
> *Obviously, it is NOT intended for carrying if flying off on holiday; airports will take a very dim view on such a bag!*

Maybe even create a personalised EDC bag for each family member? Filled with appropriate items tailored to each family member's own preferences and individual needs. Obviously, age-appropriate content.

While there are lots of online retailers selling ready assembled bags, sometimes, it adds to the learning process for you to personally select which items are relevant to your individual needs. In addition, by buying each item separately, you can select what quality and grade of each product you want. Most pre-assembled bags use more budget-priced contents to hit a retail price point.... This is not the ideal scenario to have a survival bag full of average or even poor quality products! For instance, my personal EDC bag cost me over £150 (My Leatherman tool was around £100 on its own), whereas you can easily find EDC bags advertised for £20 or £30.... it's your decision on what quality, what investment, and what value you place on your own and your families wellbeing in an emergency scenario. Do not forget that if you end up replying and using this stuff, there may not be any stores left open to replace poor quality items that have quickly failed and broken.

My role in writing this book is to help you achieve a suitable level of preparedness so that you can best protect your loved ones....my aim is not to sell you loads of products; I suggest you carefully look at my bags content kit lists, then make based on this, your own list of everything you want to buy, and do some online research to study price comparisons. Amazon and E bay have it covered.

Your EDC Bag(s). everyday carry bag. I have 3 different EDC bag versions I regularly use. Each is selected dependent upon where I am going and what I am doing. Create your own personal favourite contents kit list, but here are my preferences on contents to think about, including.
Also, please visit my web site www.Dingo-Preppers.co.uk *to view full information and the most up to date info, etc.*

BAG 1: My all-time favourite carry is my small leather belt bag; this only holds really key essentials: -
My Leatherman for Multi-Tool and Knife: - Leatherman-skeletool-CX
Torch for light
Petrol Lighter to create fire for heat/warmth etc. and a few plasters for minor cuts

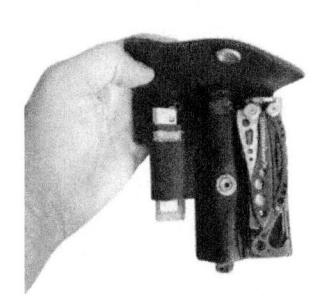

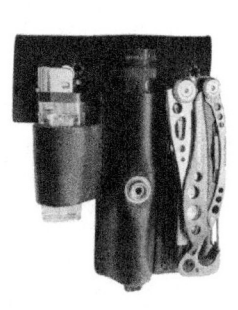

(NB. *My Leatherman may not strictly pass our UK knife laws because the blade whilst only very small, the blade locks in place, and locking knives are considered illegal in the UK to carry around. So I always advise you to double-check any equipment you buy and intend carrying that it is legal. At 57, I expect I would get away with a warning if stopped. If I was a teenager, it might be looked on more seriously; enough said*!)

BAG 2: My Medium leather belt bag, this only holds far more key items, a good mid-range EDC option: -
My Leatherman for Multi-Tool and Knife: - Leatherman-skeletool-CX
Torch for light

Petrol Lighter to create fire for heat/warmth etc.
A bandage and a few plasters for minor cuts
Some mini light glow sticks
An emergency foil "Space Blanket."
A length of paracord

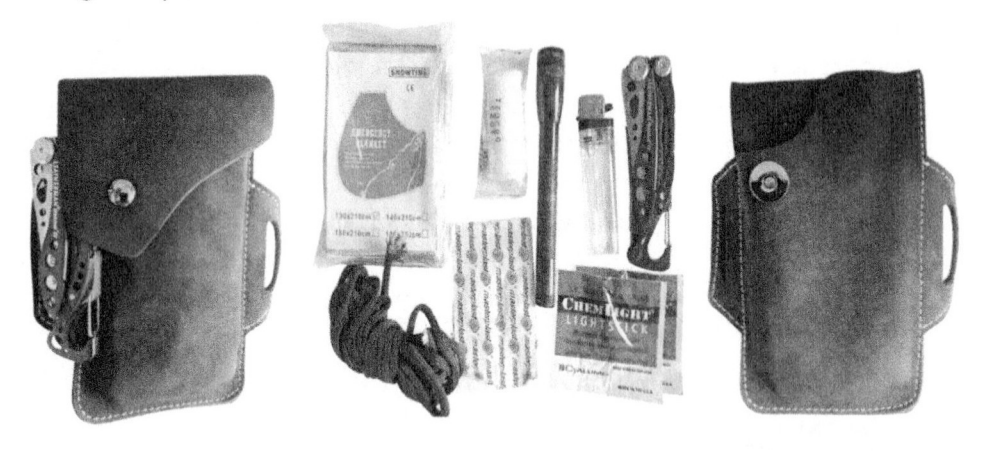

BAG 3: This is my MAIN EDC Bag
it holds the most comprehensive range of key items
I use a small shoulder bag (*about £20 off auction sites*), it's NOT a big bag at all, but I think you will be very surprised by all it can hold. Dimensions: H23 x W16 x D8 and capacity: 3L

His N Hers Mini Shoulder Crossbody bags (Approx. GB £20 each)

I have listed every single thing I carry in this bag. However, it is important to understand that different situations will benefit you if you have some of the content, but often, not all the content. For instance, mountain hiking will need some of the contents, but naturally, you will not need to take everything with you, so it's vital to be aware of where you are going and plan ahead all possible events and pack anything you deem useful.

This bag for me has taken 30 years of tweaking, adding to, and removing from, based upon my own life events and situations I have encountered. I think that this now has the **ultimate EDC bag contents list**…. Remember travelling and airport restrictions…. Do not carry as your hand luggage!

Kit list contents
Fire Starting Kit (+cotton wool balls)
Disposable Lighter
2 x Emergency Foil Space Blankets
2 x Toothbrush and toothpaste
Hand Sanitiser (70% Alcohol content)
Pocket tissue Pack
Travel Toilet Paper Roll
3 x Surgical 3 Ply Face Masks
Bandanna (face mask/injury pad)
Emergency Food Rations: IE Kendal Mint Cake bars/Dexol Tablets
4 x Water Purification Tablets
LED Tiny Rechargeable Flashlight
Head Band Light
Survival Whistle
Compass
Writing Note Pad, Pen (pen with glass breaker/defence tip)
Chemical Light Sticks – NATO Military Grade
Mobile Phone power-bank charger back up battery and charging cables
Multi-tool
Paracord Rope length
PVC Tape Roll
Travel Sewing kit

Cable Ties selection
Mini First Aid Kit and Bandages/Safety Pins/ Tourniquet / Eye Wash Drops/Safety Pins set
Medications and antiseptics.... aspirin/paracetamol/anti-diarrhoea tablets
CPR Face Mask
1 x Midges / Mosquito Head Net
Multi Tool: - Leatherman-skeletool-CX
Small Pocket Knife (*Legal UK carry*) SEE
https://www.amazon.co.uk/s?k=uk+legal+pocket+knifeandref=nb_sb_noss
(SEE **INDEX 2** Re UK knife laws)
+
Identification (photocopies and ideally laminated for protection from the elements)
Cash
Mobile Phone

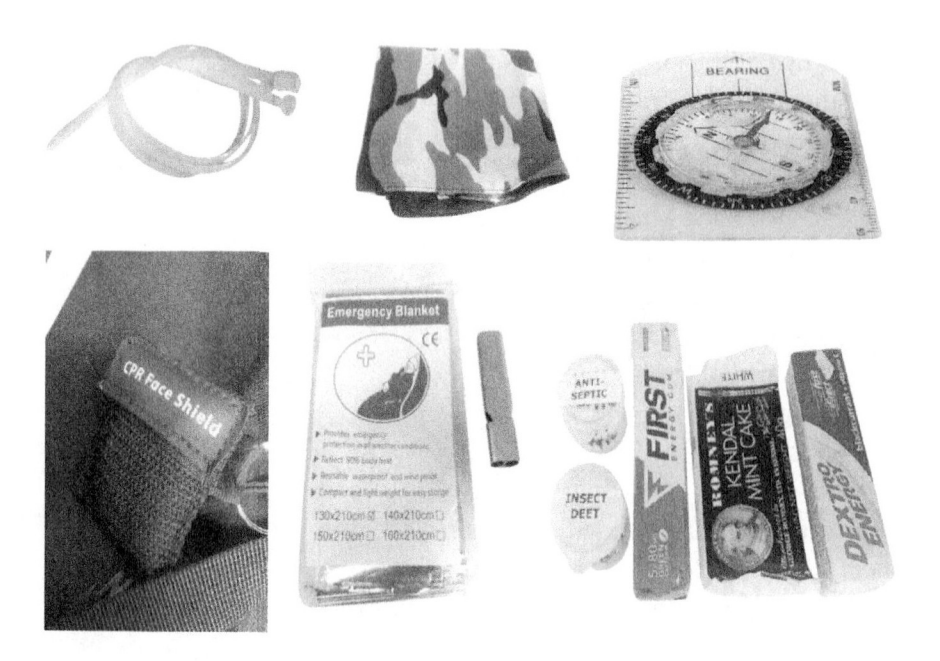

47

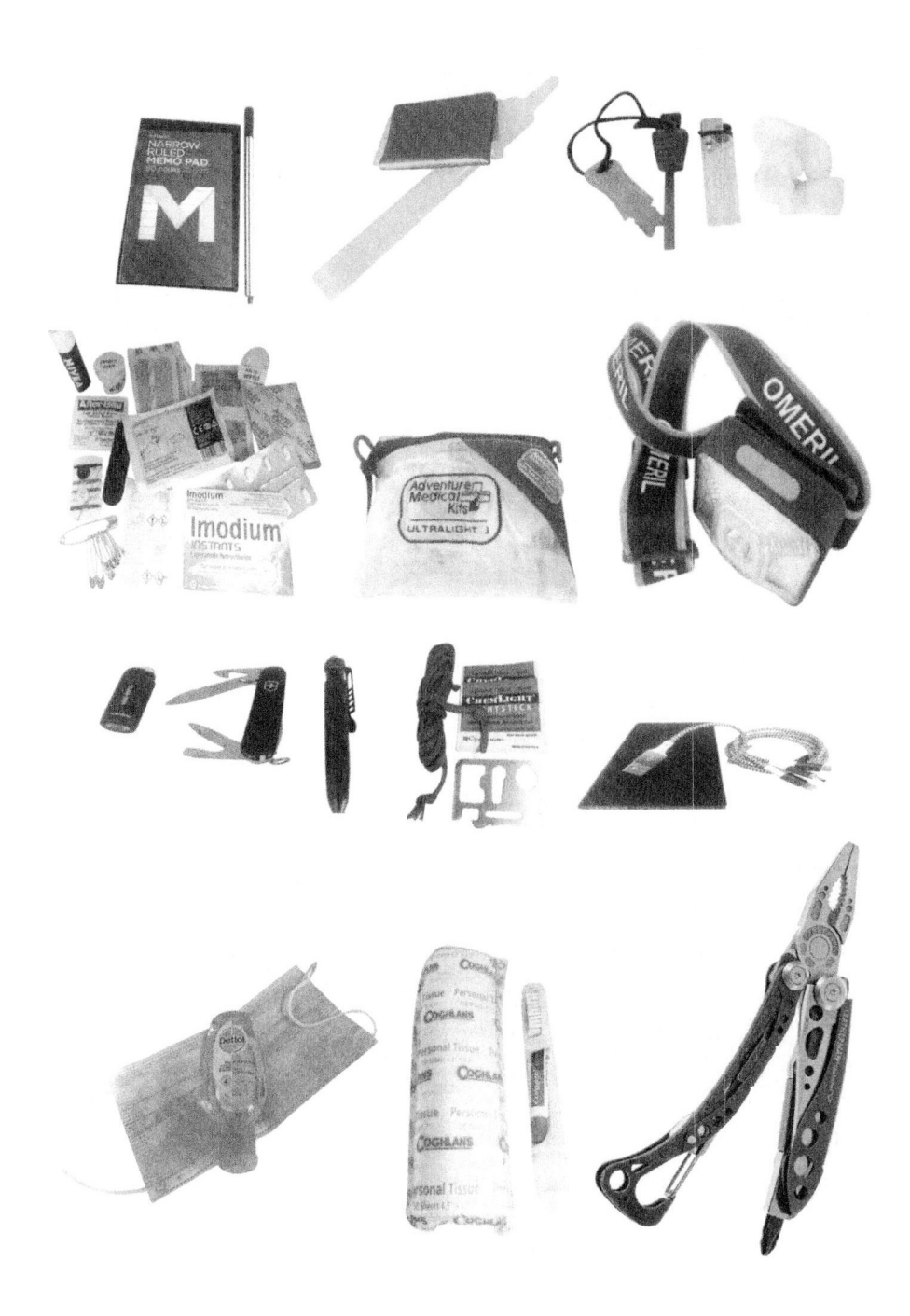

CHAPTER 6

Step 3: Home Security and Home Defence

> TOP TIP and KEY POINT to make you far more aware of how safe and secure, or how vulnerable your home actually is to being broken into and simple steps to improve your security and safety.

Already, with your new food and water supplies stockpiled, you are now more prepared than 99% of the population, plus I bet you are feeling far more confident in your ability to be better prepared for yourself and your loved ones. However, it would be foolhardy of me not to point out another key area which needs your earliest consideration….

DEFENDING YOUR HOME

Sadly, if things ever get really bad and food shortage is out of control, then expect to get people or gangs wanting to get their hands on your supplies AT ANY COST….
Commonly referred to as SHTF (S*** hits the fan)

Once looting begins, civil unrest, violence, and attacks will occur within 3 weeks after the food supply stops reaching supermarkets.
If you have food and water, then other survivors will want to take it off you. FACT.
Imagine if you were not prepared with food and water supplies and your family were hungry, what would you do? **No, seriously...what would you do?** Not nice to think of, is it? If you answered honestly, your answer would be that you would do almost anything necessary to feed and keep your family safe...But remember, so will everyone else.

It is a documented fact that under these conditions, humans quickly change and soon turn feral and aggressive when needed. Usually, the first reaction to a major disaster is shock, disbelief, and some sense of community. Closely followed by panic and violence at varying levels. At this point, unless our government/military can intervene to restore order quickly, then the population will quickly turn to increased violence. Riots, looting, attacks against neighbours and home invasions, etc.

If you want to be freaked out with details, then try a read of David Georges small book "UK Prepping" (see my reading bibliography list in the Index). It makes for dark reading.

In my opinion, I believe the UK is actually a very safe and friendly country for the general population. Although our government may have made some poor and slow decisions during the COVID-19 pandemic, overall, they rapidly restored food supplies and vastly increased medical facilities but had it exceeded the power of our National Health Service (NHS) and governments ability to take control, then the outcome would have gotten out of control for most citizens and who knows what impact this could have had on everyone and our access to food and supplies.

Still in doubt? Do you still have the "won't happen to me" mindset...? Remember Hurricane Katrina in New Orleans. Whilst a lot of the stories about lawlessness and looting were exaggerated, looting 100% did occur, and people did die. It needed the national guard's arrival before safety, and public order was eventually restored. These are those vital days or weeks when you and your family are <u>most at risk</u>. That time period between disaster and sufficient help and fresh supplies arriving. These are the periods and time frames when you may be in most need of a damn good home defence plan to protect your stockpiles of food, water, and other key essentials.

Won't ever happen though in the UK though, you think????
https://en.wikipedia.org/wiki/2011_England_riots
The **2011 riots of England**, more widely known as the London Riots, were a series of riots between 6 and 11 August 2011. Thousands of people rioted in cities and towns across England, which saw looting, arson, mass deployment of police, and the deaths of five people.

Let me ask you this…. are you happy and absolutely 100% confident that whatever may befall your country, that your government, police, and emergency services will <u>always</u> be able to step in and keep you and your family safe at all times? Fine, in that case, don't waste your time prepping then.
Or would you rather have some personal say and some personal control over your own safety and your family's needs?
Because you are reading this book, I think I already know your answer. So with that in mind, and without getting into the very advanced preps of bug-out locations at this stage, let's look at how you can better protect your home in such times of worst-case scenarios. In my opinion, it is far better to have this awareness and knowledge before things go bad. This way, you are better able and better prepared to defend your home, your family, and your supplies should looters come knocking.

Here's just a brief outline of things for you to consider in making your home safe from looters and attacks.

- Split your food/water supplies. Ideally, spread out your cache, so in case of looters, for example, you may be forced to flee your home.

When you return, if all your food was in one room, then for sure, it's all being taken.

- **Here's a list of 6 great tips**: -
  These six are definitely worth considering
  1. Loft Attic Space: Most looters would go straight to your kitchen for your food supplies, harder to reach loft spaces would largely be overlooked, especially if there was not an easy ladder to pull down (hint hint)
  2. I'm a big fan of beds with hydraulic arms, giving you massive under bed storage. You would be amazed at how much food can fit underneath a standard double bed. Yet, the bed still looks just like a regular bed, again easily overlooked by looters.
  3. Underfloor cavities, behind wardrobes, etc. Anywhere you can create a hidden secret cache storage area.
  4. Bury supplies in air and watertight containers in your back garden. For a large and serious cache, one of the best choices is to utilise a new plastic septic tank for this purpose.
  5. Buy a good stock of candles for light if the power grid goes down. I'm not a big fan of using generators during times when things are so bad that looters are raiding homes and shops. A generator is noisy and needs ventilation, thus, making your home a very noticeable place. Instead, ensure your window blinds and curtain are blackouts to stop the light shining through. This way, when you are using your candles, your home will not become a lighthouse and draw in the looters like a beacon from miles around! Stealth is key; you do not ever want to draw attention to yourselves or especially your supplies.
  6. Plan and agree with your family about an <u>emergency evacuation plan</u>, with locations for up to 3 different rendezvous points (RV). Should your family become separated or are all out at different locations when suddenly a disaster strikes, each family member will know to go straight to RV point 1; if this is compromised, maybe people are already there, etc., they can move onto RV 2, etc. Ideally and in secrecy, bury here some key back up supplies in

case you are forced to flee your home or if family members reach each RV point and need some urgent supplies just to keep them going. You may also want to invest in a set of 2-way walkie talkies, a great way to keep in contact with your family if you get separated over a short distance (Remember, mobile phone networks may be down and phones will no longer be working). Add these into the emergency RV caches.

- Install CCTV and sensor lights. Only viable if power and Wi-Fi uninterrupted, but home security basics like these, in my opinion, should be installed regardless of everyday security.

- Beneath all low-level windows plant bushy and spikey plants such as roses with big thorns. You want to deter looters in every way possible. Even simple subtle deterrent can be very effective but are also discreet and harmless looking.

- Buy several battery-operated motion sensor alarms, plus have a stock of spare batteries. Place these all around the approaches to your house, including your back garden, pathways, patios, fences.
As a back-up method, try some old school fishing line strung across various locations and attached to piles of tin cans, etc., so you will be pre-warned when there is commotion.

- Fit best quality deadbolts and locks, making sure your door lock has a bolt that goes at least an inch into the door frame complete with a metal strike plate (the part that holds the bolt) and is secured in place by 3" long screws. Is your front and back door solid enough to withstand being kicked in? Fit better quality doors, non-glazed types (*solid steel being best. Sorts drug dealers install to slow down police raid entry!*), windows, locks, etc. these will "give you time" in the event of an attack. Let's face it, if they want to get in, they will.... but many of these measures are to give you time to react and mount a defence and launch any counter-attacks.

For instance, during my robbery, I had solid oak doors, 5 lever good quality door locks, all windows were fitted with locks too. How did they break in, you ask? They smashed their way through the patio windows. As I've said, if they want to get in, they will...all we can do is slow them down, this will enable you have sufficient time to phone the police, mount a defence, get your family together and easier to protect, time to barricade all of your family in one room together...time is key.

In my situation, my Krav Maga instincts kicked in on autopilot, no sense of being a hero I simply responded the way my Krav training had taught me. The attackers were not expecting one old guy to take on 5 armed attackers; it put them off their game just enough. Now I have added CCTV, Sensor lights, and now my glass patio door is triple glazed with an added security film which is like plastic sandwiched between the glazing. This takes a lot more time and effort to get through....precious time for me to wake up, call the police, or start my counter-attack. Time is the best outcome that any of these home defences can give you.

- You can buy security window film, as mentioned above, to cover all window glazing, making smashing a way in harder and more time-consuming. A few random suppliers are shown below from a quick Google search: - *I do not receive any financial incentive from these supplies listed. They are examples of suppliers only. Best to search for your local supplier.*
  Info video:- https://www.youtube.com/watch?v=NRmpPnP9Ekc
  Examples Installers: -
  https://supira.co.uk/window-film/safety-security-film/
  https://www.windowfilm.co.uk/residential/security

- There are some great and often inexpensive devices available online, from simple door wedges, letterbox locks (*to stop petrol being poured through letter flap to smoke you out the house*) and window vibration alarms, to window shutters, and even security roll-down shutters. The better the system, sadly often the uglier the device, i.e., roll

down shutters. So your partner will need to be fully on board with whichever options you choose to install.
Door Jammers, Window Locks, Letterbox locks
https://www.amazon.co.uk/s?k=Door+Jammersandref=404_search

Funnelling

(*You will learn more about this if you take up Krav Maga or similar self-defence training*). In the case of an attack, you need to think about how to funnel multiple attackers into a single file. Taking them on one-to-one is far easier than five-to-one! In most houses, this means staging your defence from the top of the stairs. You have the high ground, and they are restricted in how many can come up the stairs at a time. You might not like to think of attacking another person, but often in these types of situations, it is to kill or be killed. Also, your family is upstairs, and you are the only thing between them and the attackers. So what can you do? Perhaps you can position a bookcase at the top of your landing, a nice piece of furniture doesn't look dangerous…now tip it down the stairs along with anything else you can lay your hands on. Barricade yourself upstairs or at least further to slow down the attackers from reaching you.
Weapons…most people will feel uncomfortable about using a knife, axe, crowbar, baseball bat, garden fork, etc. against another person…. but this is the reality of having the right mind-set to fully defend your home and family whatever it takes. Obviously, some of these are only for the very extreme end of home defence and only realistic if law and order have completely broken down, and everyone's out for themselves with no emergency services and support to call upon…

Another way of funnelling is to creatively force attackers or looters along a route of your choice. Humans are lazy by nature, so if large thorny roses or strategically placed garden furniture and obstacles are placed. The invaders unknowingly will follow a path following the seemingly easier route. But this is a path of your choice.

- A few other thoughts, again, to slow down attackers from gaining entry. Some of these may sound extreme, and they are not for times of minor events; these are the big events when you may have to defend your home for days or weeks at most with no support available from our police and emergency services.
Nail chicken wire over all doors and windows (if wooden frames)
Nail or deadbolt wooden planks over doors and windows
Glue locks shut
Lay planks full of nails pointing upwards, around door and window entry points, any attackers in trainers will soon discover them! (assuming by now you and your family are residing upstairs)
Buy a crossbow and lots of bolts, so you can defend your home from the upstairs windows.
Have to hand lots of firefighting defences, fire blankets, extinguishers, plus of course, lots of smoke detectors and spare batteries. If attackers can't get in, they may try and smoke you out. You need to first try and extinguish any such fires, but you also need a back-up plan. I suggest you buy a window emergency escape ladder. Not ideal if you have to leave your home, but again it's something you need to plan for and practise using.
You would need to descend first to protect your family as they come down. Not a great scenario relying on having to fight your way past attackers, but what else can you do?

- Buy a dog, no seriously go buy a dog right now; the dog breed is a key element, however. The right dog will not only fight to its death protecting you and your family but give you three other benefits: -
    1. The presence of a large dog will deter all except the most committed attackers, after all, there will always be easier homes to attack. Those without a dog, CCTV cameras, sensor lights, etc.
    2. A dog has far better hearing than us mere humans and will always wake and alert you to danger with its barking. Dogs are very territorial and will instinctively defend your home and family.
    3. A dog will also smell fire and smoke and will often warn you well before your home smoke detector even goes off.

Personally, I would recommend a Rottweiler, Doberman, Staffordshire Pit Bull Terrier, Bull Mastiff, Rhodesian Ridgeback, Boerboel, or of course, the UK favourite Police Dog, the German Shepherd (Alsatian).

We own a Rottweiler, sadly he was only a 3-month-old puppy at the time of our house attack, but even at that age, he took a Machete blow to his head in trying to defend us…. now at 3years, he is a big 10 stone beast with a bark and growl to match. He is a superb family dog, soft and loving with us…. but try knocking our front door one day; I guarantee you would not want to try and break in…ha haaa

- WORST CASE is that you have to flee your home. It is vital for you, and most importantly, every member of your family to know the escape plan. Plan and practise getting to your chosen RV point (you need more than one RV point to meet up; I advise at least 3 in case 2 cannot be reached or are compromised). You will want to gather all your family as soon as possible, and knowing the order of places to meet up will be vital.

- If you are getting into this prepping mentality and have the right mind-set, think about burying some hidden caches of food/drink/weapons/torch/tarp for shelter building/fire starter and first aid kit. These are your key essentials to staying safe.

CHAPTER 7

Step 4: Medical Supplies and First Aid Training

TOP TIP and KEY POINT: Learn some basic first aid at an absolute minimum. Being "prepared" often means being self-reliant and not having to rely on help from others, such as our Emergency services. Our NHS and emergency services are some of the best in the world.... but, just maybe, there could be another bigger event that means they cannot be with you quickly, or even at all. You need to cope with being self-sufficient just in case.

This stage is to prepare your medical kit and knowledge. First, buy your medical supplies and next book to attend a local First Aid course (or two) for some practical hands-on learning.

Key points to consider are what's key for you and your particular family's particular needs. Any allergies or regular medications you need to stock up on, such as asthma inhalers, heart medication, insulin, contact lens, and solutions, etc. Prescription medication can be slowly "added to" each time you go to get a new prescription filled. It is normally fine to get a three-month supply from your GP (doctor), more if you say you are going away on an extended holiday.

Your simplest starting point is to buy a decent pre-packaged family-sized home first aid kit...then tweak and add to it until it fully meets your own particular needs.

> **TIP:** *Download a first aid manual on your smartphone for emergency use and reference, plus buy some laminated on how to pocket-sized guides with simple step by step first aid instructions.*

Here are some key items to consider including
but is by no means an all-inclusive list: -

Reference manual / First Aid book / Pocket Guides / Phone App:
You will need guides as this is a complex area

Feminine creams and essentials - Tampons, panty liners, and sanitary pads IE. Anti-fungal cream (Canesten) - treats yeast infections, under breast sweat rash, and ringworm.

Baby / Infant Care - Nappies, baby wipes, and nappy rash creams
Calpol is ideal for young children who have difficulty swallowing regular pills. Infant paracetamol for children

Your Pet care – Any creams, lotions, tablets that your pets may be taking. Even pet tranquillizers to keep your pets calm during an emergency evacuation.
Tick remover tool (pet & human use!) – **TIP**: Cover tick in vasoline type cream (Petroleum jelly), as this suffocates the tick. After a few minutes, use a tick tool to pull it out but do not squeeze the tick as it will squeeze its poison into the wound.

Latex or Nitrile gloves: Nitrile, in my opinion, are your best choice.
Nitrile is a synthetic rubber compound that is commonly used as a disposable glove material. Nitrile has been around for a while, but only recently it's become more affordable, which explains why it's gaining popularity

throughout medical, food, and cleaning industries. Nitrile has a higher puncture resistance than any other glove material. Nitrile also has a better chemical resistance than Latex or Vinyl gloves.

Facemasks & Hand antiseptic gels (70% alcohol content) and antibacterial soap

Body oils/ Moisturisers: To prevent dry and broken skin. Dry skin can be a trigger for eczema

Splints for broken bones

Tube of superglue: a weird but quick fit to protect and harden torn skin or close small wounds

Heat and Cooling Sprays / Muscle relief creams

EpiPen: gives a shot of adrenalin to fight life-threatening anaphylactic shock, i.e., *Bee stings, Peanut type allergies, (Usually needs a prescription to get)*

Oral Thermometer (*non-battery type*)

Anti-emetic: Good for nausea, travel sickness, feelings of wanting to vomit

Medical Hypo: allergenic Instant Wound Closure Strips Sutures

CPR masks: designed to protect against disease transmission and helps when blood, vomit, and other bodily fluids make creating an airtight seal difficult

Plasters in a variety of different sizes and shapes

Zinc Oxide tape: super sticky tape, great barrier to stop blisters forming

Alcohol-free cleansing wipes

Hydrocortisone or calendula cream: Relives rashes, eczema, insect bites, bee stings, and nappy rash.

Hay fever, Anti-histamine Tablets (Piriteze) - For allergy relief, including pet allergies, dust, and mould spores.
Bee sting and insect bite lotions

Jungle formula insect repellent: To ward off nuisance bugs and avoid an allergic reaction to bites

Anti-septic cream (Sudocream): an antibacterial cream that contains penicillin, which is good for killing bacteria that cause infections. These creams can relieve irritations on the skin and aid the healing process.

Sterile eye dressings, eye drops, eye bath, and eyewash.

Ear drops

Anti-acid for indigestion

Laxatives: Helpful for relieving constipation, softening stools, and intestinal cramping.

Anti-Diarrhoea tablets such as Imodium

Hydration Electrolyte Powders (or mix one teaspoon of salt in 1 litre of water): Remedy for heat exhaustion

Burn ointment and possibly a specialist burns treatment kit

Aspirin (Disprin): It is good for pain relief, fever, and can be used as a blood thinner, which can aid strokes and heart attacks. (NOT to be given to under 16yrs; always follow packet instructions)

Paracetamol (Nurofen): Painkillers are extremely helpful in handling minor pains and discomfort.

Anti-inflammatory (Ibuprofen): These anti-inflammatory drugs work by reducing nerve pain in the body, such as toothache, back pain, and arthritis.

Pseudoephedrine (Sudafed), ideal for chest and nasal congestion, cold, and flu symptoms.

Cough medication

Chapped lips cream

Sterile gauze pads, dressings, and roll and compression bandages, including triangular bandages

Blood pressure monitors

Glucose blood sugar testing (if battery operated get spare batteries too)

Tourniquets

Scissors & tweezers, plus some safety pins

Metal unbreakable mirror (to help treat facial cuts, for example, if you are on your own. Doubles up as a signal mirror)

Petroleum jelly

Cotton Swabs

Distilled water to wash out wounds and irrigation syringe (to wash out cuts and wounds)

Ipecac bottle (to induce vomiting in case swallowed something poisonous)

Sun Cream and after sun.

Cold sore cream

Mouth ulcer cream

Emergency aluminium space-blankets

A suture kit to stitch up wounds and sewing needles

Quick Clot - Blood clotting trauma care for the more severe emergencies

A trauma wound dressing sometimes called an Israeli Bandage for deeper wounds

Finally, you may also want to add into your kit dependent on space and your level of medical skill: -
Multivitamins / Minerals tablets, stethoscope to help verify breathing and heartbeat, as well as some respiratory issues, cervical collar to immobilise neck/spine injuries, blood pressure cuff

I strongly advise you to attend a couple of first aid courses, too, especially one which covers CPR.
In the UK the St John Ambulance runs many courses for all levels.
To be fully prepped, you must always think self-sufficiency, try and imagine what you would do if you do not have access to doctors and hospitals, etc. This goes for your veterinarian pet care too!

Shelf-Life
It is always best to have fresh medical supplies to hand; however, most, BUT NOT ALL, drugs can be stored 5 years past their expiry date if kept in an airtight container and stored correctly in a cool, dry place.

Boots and Blisters

(Good quality waterproof boots are <u>essential</u>)

The proverb says, "prevention is better than cure." In a prepper/survival situation that could also require you to "Bug Out" to a safer location, you need to consider a few fundamental basics: -

1. Good quality boots, waterproof walking boots are ideal. If you are a hiker or dog walker, you know what I am about to say…. BREAK IN YOUR BOOTS, its vital you have comfortable boots if you intend walking any kind of distance! The very last thing you want, in an already stressful situation, are blisters to contend with too, and new boots with little or no mileage on them are blister magnets.

2. Break in your boots. Obviously, the best approach is to wear them for many miles, so they soften and mould to the shape of your feet. Like the days gone by, when folk of my age will remember wearing a pair of new jeans in the bath to get them to shrink to fit (Yes, we really did that back in the day, this was pre-stretch denim times!), but I digress…the same idea works with your new leather boots. This tip is for leather boots, not modern technical materials. Put your leather boots on and lace them up, then stand in a bowl of hot water till the leather soaks up some of the water. Now walk around in them until they dry up; this will help them mould to the shape of your feet.

3. Blisters…. A really simple ailment to avoid, but surprisingly painful if you get them. In any survival situation, strong, healthy feet are essential for getting you around (ask any soldier about the importance of healthy feet). That said, knowing how to treat them is as important as knowing how to avoid them. The main defence is to wear good quality hiking socks, and if they get wet, change them, giving your feet a good dry and a coating of talcum powder for dry and freshness. Always change damp, wet, or sweaty socks as these will dramatically increase your risk of blisters.

4. When walking, if you feel a tingly hot spot on your feet, that's your early warning of a potential blister. Do not continue, stop, and treat it immediately. The easiest cure is to apply some Zinc Oxide tape; this super sticky tape is well tough and is great to apply strips of on heels, toes, etc., anywhere your boots are rubbing and leaving tell-tale redness signs.

5. Too late...you have got a blister! To pop or not, that old-age question. Ideally, you would never choose to pop your blister because the liquid inside is sterile and has formed to protect the wound below. But in a survival situation, you can't stop and wait for it to recover, so best to pop it. Sterilise a needle or sharp tip of your knife over a flame from a lighter. Now gently ease out the liquid being careful not to tear the skin bubble as this protects the wound below. It is vital you look after your feet, so keep the blister super clean and check it regularly. Ideally, use a dab of antiseptic cream to help prevent infection. Clean, dry socks are also essential.

6. Keep a careful eye out for redness, swelling, or even infected pus seeping out. Regular cleaning and inspection will help you avoid this.

7. WEIRD TIP: - From my days of rock climbing, I often used to squirt some superglue onto any torn skin on my fingers; it burns a little but hardens into a strong protective layer. A superb option to repair torn skin on your blister. (Not that your local doctors would endorse such a practise, but we are in survival mode here)

Tourniquets

Recommended covering tourniquets as part of your first aid training course choice

The use of tourniquets is a bit of a controversial topic. There are some pros and cons to using them or not! Being in a survival situation, you need a tourniquet in your first aid preps.

Having a catastrophic bleed, usually from a major wound or even a severed limb, will need the use of a tourniquet to stop the blood flow.

If a tourniquet is used when it's not a major bleed, the patient could well lose the limb as the tourniquet will cut off the blood flow and can cause the limb to die. In these lesser wounds, although still, super-serious direct pressure is the way to go to stop further blood loss.

However, in a survival situation, to treat a severed limb or to stop major blood loss using a tourniquet is your only option.

- If the wound is on a thigh or upper arm, position the tourniquet at least 5cms above it
- For below elbow or knee wounds, the tourniquet should be positioned just above the knee or elbow joint.
- Now tighten the tourniquet really tight, tighter than you would think regardless of the screams from your patient. You must stop the bright red arterial blood from flowing. You may still see some dark red venous blood oozing through, though.
- You may need to re-tighten the tourniquet if the limb starts to become less swollen.
- Unless the tourniquet is positioned at the end of a severed limb, in this case, do not remove or loosen it. But if the wound is not a sever or amputation, release it every fifteen minutes to allow the blood to flow to the limb to keep it healthy.

DIY: Stitching up a wound

An open wound, whilst it may not immediately be life-threatening, if it doesn't get sorted out, it can get infected, and then it could become life-threatening.

What type of wound may need stitching...?

- Any cut more than an inch long
- A cut you can't get the sides to close up when taped with gaffa tape, or even superglue (*my personal favourite and more sterile than stitching*)
- A wound that will not stop bleeding, even after heavy pressure applied
- You can see muscle or bone through the cut

Options in a survival situation....
Obviously, a suture kit is a key item for inclusion in your Bug Out medical kit Other survival stitching thread options could be dental floss and fishing line. You still need a needle, or at a push a small fishing hook, and do not forget to sterilise it first in boiling water, washed in alcohol, or sterilised in a lighter's flame. Thoroughly wash the wound, ensure no debris or dirt remains in the wound, which could cause infection.

Stitch using a continuous line, don't stitch too deep; you only need to sew into the layer just below the skin. Try not to use too many stitches. Firstly, each one can invite infection, and secondly, they have to come out at some point, which can be painful.

BROKEN BONES: Definitely to be avoided in a survival situation.
This is a massively complex area, really only sufficiently covered by professional and extreme trauma medical training. In short, I strongly advise NOT to break a limb whilst there are no medical facilities to call upon!
The first priority is to establish if it's an open (bone poking through the skin stuff) or a closed fracture. Closed fractures can be just as nasty because shards of broken bone internally can cut into arteries and veins, resulting in internal bleeding.

An open fracture where the bone is poking through the skin has a high chance of bleeding and infection. If the wound is bleeding, apply direct pressure and rinse it off with sterile water before putting a dressing on it. Try to flush out any dirt and debris; don't scrub or rub the area.
Use traction to pull the exposed bone ends back in place; the bones may return below the skin surface when traction is applied. Then apply a splint to hold the limb in place.

DISLOCATED BONES
Extremely painful, but can be fixed yourself if absolutely no access to professional medical help, and you have a high pain threshold. All first aid manuals will advise against trying to fix it yourself due to potential damage to blood vessels, muscles, ligaments, and nerves, but in a survival situation with no access to medical help, what other options do you have.

Reduction or "setting" is resetting the bones back into their proper alignment. You can use several methods, but manual traction (pulling) or the use of weights to pull the bones back into place are the safest and easiest. Once completed, reduction quickly decreases the pain and allows for normal function and circulation. Without access to proper medical facilities and an X-ray, you can judge the proper alignment by the look and the feel of the joint and by visually comparing it to the joint on your body's opposite side.

HYPOTHERMIA:
Temperature guides are shown in Fahrenheit & Celsius
Hypothermia occurs when the human body's' core temperature falls below **96 °F /** 35.5 °C. Symptoms include uncontrollable shivering, drowsiness, slurred speech, and loss of coordination.
Treatment is straightforward, place the patient inside a sleeping bag, or wrap them in an emergency space blanket, skin to skin (no clothing!); naked contact quickly helps warm up the patient. A hot and sweet cuppa can help too. Be aware that it can take literally hours to fully and safely raise the body temperature sufficiently. Do NOT rub or massage the patient nor immerse them into hot water as this causes the body to move warm blood towards the skin and away from the body's core, where it is more vitally needed.
WEIRD TIP: encourage the patient to urinate; the body actually uses a lot of heat energy in keeping urine warm in your bladder

HYPERTHERMIA
Temperature guides are shown in Fahrenheit & Celsius
Defined as a temperature greater than **99.5–100.9 °F /** 37.5–38.3 °C
Hyperthermia (often thought of as heat stroke or heat exhaustion) is a heat-related condition characterised by an abnormally high body temperature; in other words, the exact opposite of hypothermia. The condition occurs when the body's heat-regulation system becomes overwhelmed by outside factors, causing a person's internal temperature to rise. In a bug out and survival situation, this could occur whilst stressed and heavily loaded, moving at speed on foot to your bug out location. I personally experienced this whilst wearing firefighter PPE and doing heavy training during a very hot summers

day; a firefighters PPE keeps heat away from the body...but also locks it inside the uniform during heavy exercise!
The accompanying dehydration can produce nausea, vomiting, headaches, and low blood pressure, and the latter can lead to fainting or dizziness. Mild effects can quickly be countered by getting into a shade, stripping off clothing, drinking lots of water (to replace lost electrolytes from sweating, mix a tablespoon of salt into a litre of water), soaking a towel and wrapping a person in it and ideally full immersion into cold water.

FROSTBITE
This helps to be aware of, but it is not a big risk here in the UK unless your location is high on a Scottish mountain.
Frostnip will occur first, signs being having your fingers and toes turning white and feeling numb. Immediately, get out of the wind, rain, or snow and gently start the rewarming process.
The best option is to warm yourself is in the armpits or groin of a "very" good friend...

Frostbite is more serious and occurs when human tissue begins to freeze in exposure to extremely cold temperatures. Frostbite usually affects extremities such as the nose, ears, fingers, and toes. Mild effects can be easily treated with warm water. It is always best practise to slowly warm up the body parts and not use direct heat from being too close to your campfire, for instance. In extreme cases, the flesh can die and turn black and may require the affected area to be amputated. The rewarming from frostbite is excruciatingly painful.

> ***TIP:*** *Never attempt to re-warm frostbite if its likely to get refrozen; this can damage the flesh beyond the point of recovery. Best leave it and wait until you reach safety and be more controlled and in stable conditions.*

CPR: Cardiopulmonary Resuscitation
Recommended as part of your first aid training course content, the action is different for children than adults.
A proper course will go through the latest CRP advice, including "Agonal Breathing" plus using various types of defibrillators too.

In basic terms, check first for a pulse by placing two fingers in the grove of the patient's neck; if no pulse detected, you need to get the patient's heart pumping by using the heel part of your hand on their chest, and you need to get air in their lungs, pinch their nose closed and breath into their mouth. All whilst keeping rhythm with The Bee Gees, Staying Alive, Staying Alive.

Don't get tired and give up; people have managed to come back well after half an hour CRP.

Three elements make up adult CRP.

1. You have a non-breathing patient

2. You need to make 30 chest compressions

3. Then you need to make 2 rescue breaths…. repeat.

CHAPTER 8

Step 5: "Bug Out Bags" and "Get Home Bags"

> **TOP TIP and KEY POINT** You may well think this is something that you will never ever need. Let's hope you are right! In case you're not, though, let's look at what sort of things go into this bag....Most items will double up as a good set of camping kit essentials anyway.....Plus, it might save your life one day.

This is what most people think about when prepping. It's a pre-packed bag, left always filled and easily available to hand. A bag that you can quickly grab and leave with during sudden unexpected emergencies. Maybe natural disasters are approaching, floods, earthquakes, rioting, etc. Typically, you have enough for you and your family to survive for at least 72 hours, along with any necessary maps to get you to your bug out location, especially if SatNav and mobile phone reception is lost. *(Not a dissimilar concept to having ready your pregnancy, birth bag ready and waiting for that sudden rush to the hospital!)*

Mine is probably more filled than most Bug Out Bags.... I like the idea of having some home comforts in there too, despite not being essentials. That said, it is VITAL you can physically carry it and cope with the weight comfortably, and for whatever distance away your Bug Out location is situated. In addition, you still need to be able to move at speed and with some agility for getting over walls, gates, fences, or even barricades. If your bag is too heavy, you will not get far, and if confronted by, for example, others wanting to take your stuff, you need enough mobility to be able to defend yourself and your partner or family. Please read my section on wearing a super-strong scaffolders type of belt; this holds absolute key vital essential items on it. This always stays with you even if, God forbid, you have to leave your main bug out bag behind in favour of speed or stealth, for instance, being chased by a gang.

Two key things you MUST DO....

1. Plan where you intend bugging out to; it doesn't make sense to have your bag ready but no hideout or safe destination in mind. You need to know exactly where you are going that you feel will be safe. This could be going by car; it could be hiking into the forest and mountains. It could be as simple as several families all meeting up at one person's designated house, which is readily stockpiled with the group's supplies; great for groups of people to work together, pool resources and skills...plus safety in numbers.

> **TIP:** *Another preppers tip is to always keep your vehicle's fuel tank at least half full at all times. Most preppers carry a container of spare fuel in their vehicle too, plus a few extra supplies such as blanket, coats, boots, water, some snacks, and some old school maps too.*

2. Make several practise runs, practise actually getting to your bug out location, check the time it takes, look for potential risk hot / danger spots along the way. Also, practise using everything in your bag. For example, camp out for a few days living just out of your bug out bag. Test all the equipment, and then refine your bag...What did you not use, not like, wish you had taken, etc. Only by doing this will you end up with a perfect bag that suits you and your bug out location. In addition, by wearing and using it, you can determine how comfortable you are with its weight.

A **"Get Home Bag" OR** can also be used as a" **Secondary"** smaller and lighter **Bug Out Bag**.
This is what I usually keep in my main car. It is kept mainly in the boot of my vehicle just in case.
Commonly referred to as a Get Home Bag. The idea of this bag is it has got everything needed to "get you home" for instance, if your vehicle gets stranded miles from anywhere and there's no phone signal, or if disaster strikes whilst you are at work, and you need to quickly get home to your family
Consequently, this bag is not as comprehensive as your main bug out bag. A lot smaller and far lighter, it may suit a teenager or a partner, etc. Your main bug out bag will have the most key things; this secondary bag is a smaller version with some of the key survival essentials only.

My main BUG OUT BAG and kit List

A Bug Out bag has pretty much a single purpose: to get you from point A to point B in a safer location. This can be on foot if necessary, or by car, motorbike, cycle, or even by canoe...It all depends on your locality, where you live, and where you have chosen as your safe, secure location. Principally, this bag needs to contain water, food, first aid, shelter, and warmth. The general rule is sufficient supplies to survive for at least 3 days. Water is probably the number one requirement but is heavy to carry. I suggest 2 x 1lt bottles. The reason being you can refill one from a found water source, but it may need treating to be safe to drink, so you still have safe water in bottle 2 until such time as you can boil or add in some water-purification tablets.

It may not be safe to light a fire, as fire may give away your location. Therefore, it is best to include lots of high-calorie foods that do not require any cooking. So things like dried fruits, nuts, granola/muesli type bars, crackers and peanut butter, and even MREs can be good (These are Meals Ready to Eat – most people think military-type packs, but there are plenty available in the camping hiking markets)

Essential Belt Kit

Vital in case of a real emergency, and you lose your main bug out bag!

> **BUG OUT BAG TIP:**
> *I strongly advise you also wear a strong "scaffolders" type tough leather belt with various pouch attachments*

Google: Scaffolding Work Tool Belt; these are the sort of very heavy-duty belt I suggest, complete with pouches
Why? Imagine you are trying to Bug Out with your rucksack on, and you get attacked or chased by a gang. You may be forced to ditch your rucksack, ideally unseen, and left somewhere safe in the hope you can return and retrieve it. But regardless, you may have no option but to ditch it in order to escape with your life; running with a heavy rucksack is not ideal. Another useful tip is to always Bug Out with stealth, very quietly, and very carefully to avoid detection.

So the idea for such a belt and pouches is that you will at least be able to still have with you some extremely vital key items, these will make defence and survival hugely easier!

KEY essentials being Tool/Knife, Light to see, Heat for warmth-cooking-water-purification, and First Aid
My belt has on it: -
Knife + Leatherman multi-tool
Axe
Fire Starter
Water purification tablets
Travel-sized first aid kit
Toothbrush and toothpaste
Facemask
Fishing line set
Emergency space blanket
Tin Can Opener
Torch
Length of paracord
Small crowbar pry tool with hammer end
+ Add a Water bottle (belt type)

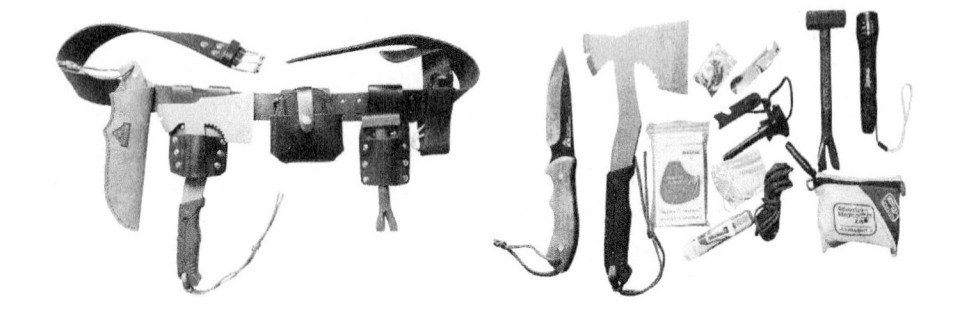

My Bug Out Bag *filled with colour coded inner kids PE sacks for fast identification and fast kit access*

*My preference rucksac is the **KARRIMOR Bobcat 65lt** size (Approx. GB £60) This bag holds a small selection of clothes plus ALL the kit in the below lists For Amazon links to my preferred kit, please visit www.Dingo-Preppers.co.uk*

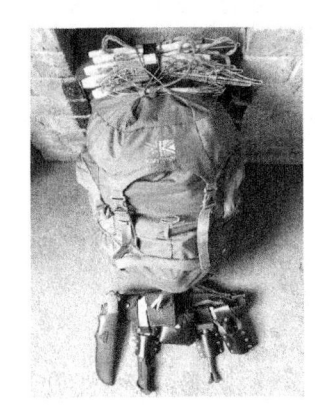

TIP: *Whatever the manufacturers might claim, NO bag is ever fully watertight. ALWAYS fit an inner "Dry Sac," some type of inner waterproof bag. Belts and braces, as my grandpa used to say....never a bad thing having a back-up, double bagged will protect your life-saving equipment!!!*

My colour code, inner bag technique.
These use simple cheap to buy kids PE sacks: -
RED – Fire equipment
ORANGE – Emergency and Safety equipment
WHITE – First Aid/Medical
BLUE – Food and Water
BLACK – Tech
GREY – Warmth, Clothing
PURPLE - Weapons/Tools
YELLOW – Bathroom, and Sanitary

RED – Fire equipment

My personal Fire starting kit is a Bayite 1/2 Inch X 6 Inch Drilled Ferrocerium Rod Flint Fire Starter together with a Light My Fire - TINDER-ON-A-ROPE – made from pine wood which comes from the highlands of Honduras, as a residual product of felled trees. It contains up to 80% resin and absorbs very little moisture. It burns extremely quickly, long and very hot (faster, hotter, and longer than paper or paraffin).
TIP: *I carry a tiny cheese grater and literally grate some of the tinder wood as the perfect fire starting tinder ever!!!! (See my Video on Twitter)*

Fire Starting Kit (cotton wool balls) + Disposable Lighters
Small Jar Petroleum Jelly *(Also a great fire starter; use it to soak your cotton wool balls)*
5 x Wax Household Candles 5hr burn
Campstove – Lightweight flat-pack type (see www.Wood-M8S.co.uk)
Cooking pans and bowls/plates/drinking mug
Sporks cutlery – *I use the metal versions as far stronger*
My personal ones are the EcoSlurps Utility Camping Spork | Stainless Steel | 5 Functions 1 Design | Fork, Knife, Spoon, Bottle Opener, Tin Opener

ORANGE – Emergency, Light, and Safety equipment

2 x Emergency Foil Space Blankets
Camping small folding lightweight Tarp
Wire Cutters *(so you can escape through wire fences)*
LED Head Torch lamp *(+ spare batteries)*
Pocket LED Light *(+ spare batteries)*
Also, consider packing a **Wind Up Torch** *(no batteries ever)*
Survival Whistle
Marine Flares *(OPTIONAL: Check laws affecting use and purchase of marine flares)*
Compass
Chemical Light Sticks – NATO Military Grade
Signal Mirror
Clear Eye Safety Wraparound Glasses Goggles
Pack of Sail Makers Needles and tough twine *(Super useful for repairing tarps, rucksacs, belts, etc.)*
Paracord or Braided Rope length *(Also some in my BLACK bag)*

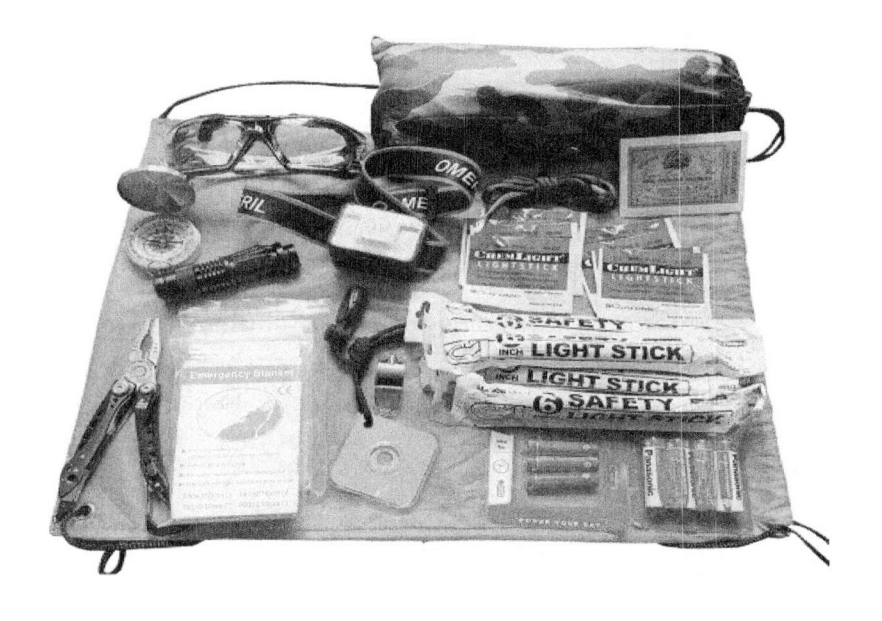

WHITE – First Aid/Medical

10 x Surgical 3 Ply Face Masks
Sam Split Roll *(This is a mouldable support for broken bones)*
Quick Clot: specialist product to deal with catastrophic bleeding injuries. *Powder or gauze form to plug into a serious wound to stem the bleeding and quickly clot the blood. Severe injury treatment!*
30-minute fire mask (Smoke filter)
First Aid Kit and Bandages/Safety Pins/ Tourniquet / Eye Wash Drops
Head Lice Comb *(let's be honest, out in the wilds, personal hygiene may be more problematic!)*
Medications and antiseptic cream…. aspirin/paracetamol/anti-diarrhoea
EpiPEN – gives a hot of adrenalin to fight life-threatening anaphylactic shock i.e., *Bee stings, Peanut type allergies, etc.*
Duct / Gaffa Tape: That strong black tape that fixes almost anything. *Its multi-use but super-useful as part of your first aid kit. It will repair bad cuts that would otherwise need stitches, strap up broken limbs onto supports, makeshift eye patch, stem bad bleeding cuts….*
Deet Insect Bug Repellent
Hand sanitiser *(TIP: this can double up as a good fire starter due to its high alcohol content)*
Small bar of soap *(for your hygiene)*
Midges / Mosquito Head Net
CPR face Mask
Sunscreen *(Burnt shoulders and a rucksac do not mix well…weather dependent!!!!)*
CONDOMS – non-lubricated condoms are a great addition to your prep bags. Not only for the obvious benefits, but they are strong enough to actually hold up to 2lts of water, an improvised glove to protect a hand or finger injury, and even a perfect sleeve to protect and keep precious fire tinder dry!

TIP: *Often overlooked, but don't forget to get Plastic Tick Removers to protect yourself and your pets whilst camping out*
Place fork under Tick - Twist in one direction until Tick remover releases and Remove - Very Simple - Pain-Free
After tick removal, cleanse the bite site with antiseptic and clean the tic tool.

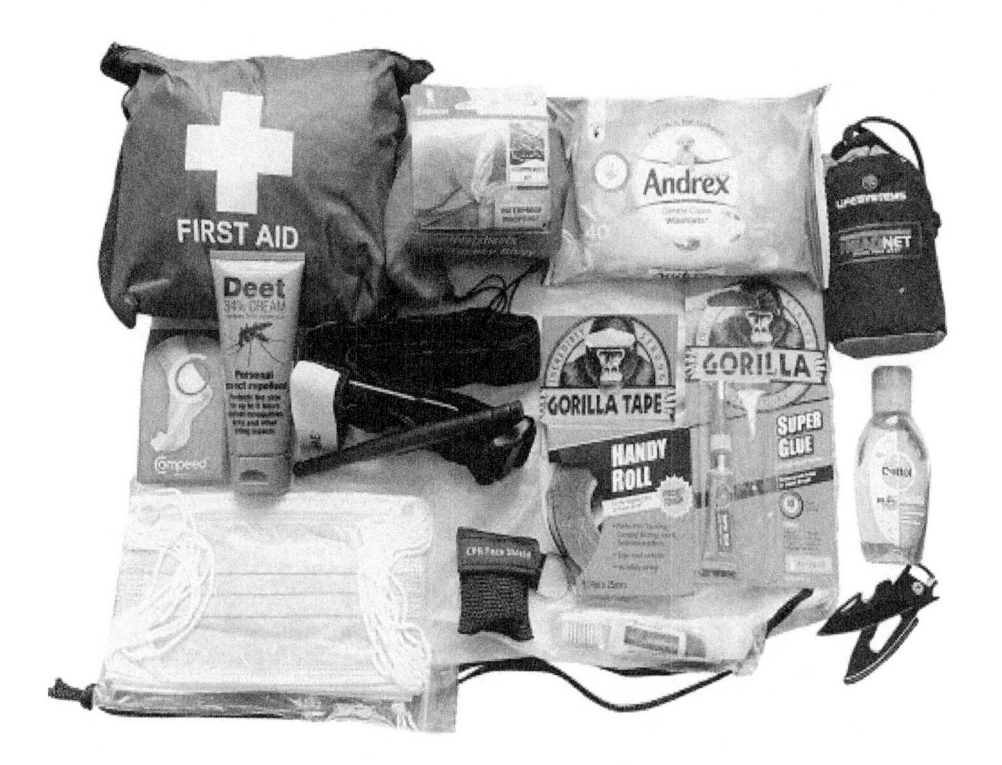

BLUE – Food and Water

2lts Water *(ideally in 2 x 1lt containers)*
Water Purification Tablets
Water Purification bottle *(self-contained water filtration bottle)*
+ or, Water Filtering Straw
Fishing line and hooks
Water drinks pouch
Food Rations: *Emergency rations and Kendal Mint Cake bars, dried fruits, nuts, granola/muesli bars*
Manual Tin Can Opener
Food foraging guide
Small hand cheese grater *(this can double up to grate dry but rotten wood, to make the best fire-starting tinder!)*
(I also have one in my Red kit pack) Sporks cutlery – *I use the metal versions as far stronger*
My personal ones are the EcoSlurps Utility Camping Spork | Stainless Steel | 5 Functions 1 Design | Fork, Knife, Spoon, Bottle Opener, Tin Opener

BLACK – Tech, Repairs, and Miscl

Do you wear glasses? Pack a spare pair
Do you wear a hearing aid? Pack spare batteries
Got a pet? Add a folding pet bowl and walking leash
Travel Sewing kit
Tube of superglue *(multi-use including small wound closure)*
Writing Note Pad, Pen and Pencil *(Use your knife to sharpen)*
Cash
Identification *(laminated photocopies to protect from the elements)*
3 strong bin bags
Pocket Survival Guide
Pair small Binoculars
Phone Waterproof DryPac case
Paracord or Braided Rope length
Gadgets and Caribana clips
PVC Tape Roll / Gaffa Tape
2 x Straps
Syphon Pump
Portable solar battery charging device
Cable Ties
"S" Hooks for hanging kit up with
Plastic Bottle Cutter to create strong cordage *(This small wooden gadget can turn discarded plastic bottles into super survival cordage. With a flame from your fire, melt the cordage after, using it to create a super-strong bond)*

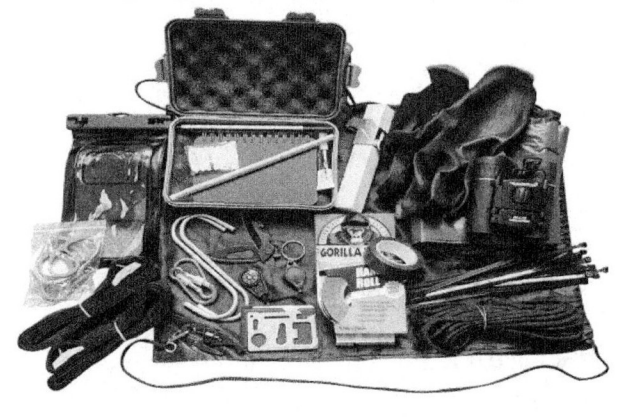

PURPLE - Weapons/Tools

Hammer and Door Pry-Lever tool *(mines on my Bug Out Scaffolders belt)*
Hammer Multi-Tool - *Alpinewolf Stainless Steel 16-in-1 Portable Multi-Functional*
Knife Sharpening Stone
Hand Auger Scotch Drill *(helps make a great Rocket Stove Fire: see fire-starting section)*
Hunting Knife NON-LEGAL CARRY (SEE INDEX 2 Re UK knife laws)
Advise full Tang blade knife i.e., *a blade that goes all way up to the end of the handle for added strength*
For UK Legal Carry Knives SEE
https://www.amazon.co.uk/s?k=uk+legal+pocket+knifeandref=nb_sb_noss
Axe and or, Machete (*or both*)
Folding Wood Saw – *I carry 2, a tube flat-pack saw, and a Gerber Bear Grylls wood saw*

Multitool (*Leatherman brand is my personal preference*)
Paracord (*550 paracord is widely used and very popular*) **or Braided Rope**
Cable Ties selection
Pocket Chainsaw
Pen with Defence/Glass breaking tip
Folding army type shovel/pick *(all in one tool) I use an Edealing Military Folding Shovel*
Small Kraft Knife (SEE **INDEX 2** Re UK knife laws)

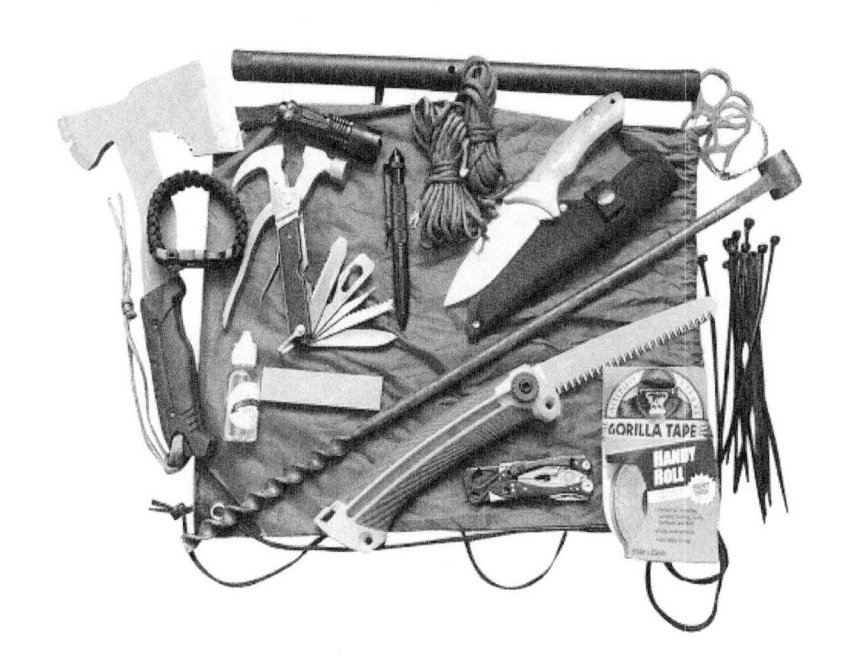

OPTIONAL extra kit to consider
Extra Weapons: Catapult/ Air Rifle / Air Pistol / Crossbow
Hand-cranked phone charger and or a portable solar charger
Hand-cranked torch
Hand-cranked AM/FM radio so you can listen to emergency radio broadcasts, which could provide situational updates.
Shortwave Radio: For more direct and advanced communications, I suggest you invest in a Shortwave Radio as this will even enable you to scan the airways and be in communication with other survivors.
Night Vision Goggles: Remember, if you need to Bug Out after the electricity grid has already gone down, there will be no street lights or lit buildings. Torches and lanterns will quickly draw you possibly unwanted attention. Night Vision goggles are the perfect accessory to either keep a watch out for looters trying to break into your home or to enable you to lead your family to your safe bug out location. They will even work if driving your car, motorbike, or campervan without the need to turn on your headlights!

GREY – Rain, Clothing, and Sleeping

Reusable Rain Poncho
Sleeping Bag and waterproof outdoor bivvy bag
Insulated Camping Mat or self-inflating mattress
OR, consider using a lightweight hammock. *This has the added advantage of raising you off an often cold, damp, and uncomfortable ground.*
Small Tarp: *Great multi-use item, ideal for helping build a simple shelter fast and making it watertight*
2 x Bandannas *(Face wrap/injury pad)*
+ or, Shemagh scarf – *bigger than a bandana at approx. 40" sq. and very useful as a head wrap, scarf, carry pouch, even a crude water filter if necessary. Some great videos online about using and wearing these*
IE https://www.youtube.com/watch?v=UHeftATdsk4
Work Gloves
Lightweight Medium-Sized Microfibre Travel Towel
Warm Baselayer Tee/Leggings/hat/gloves
Set Hiking Lightweight and waterproof Clothes
OPTIONAL Martial Art forearm protectors/Shin Leg protection/Helmet/Knuckle gloves/Box (groin protection) etc. (Specialty equipment to help protect you in attacks and confrontations)
OPTIONAL Knife Slash proof clothing, Kevlar lined clothing for added body protection

YELLOW – Bathroom, and Sanitary

2 x Toothbrush and toothpaste
Wet Wipes
2 x Tissue packs
Travel Toilet Paper Roll *(or standard toilet roll, remove card tube, crush flat)*
2nd Small Microfibre Travel Towel
Concentrated Travel Wash
Small bar of soap
Hand Sanitiser (70% alcohol) – *also makes a great fire starter*

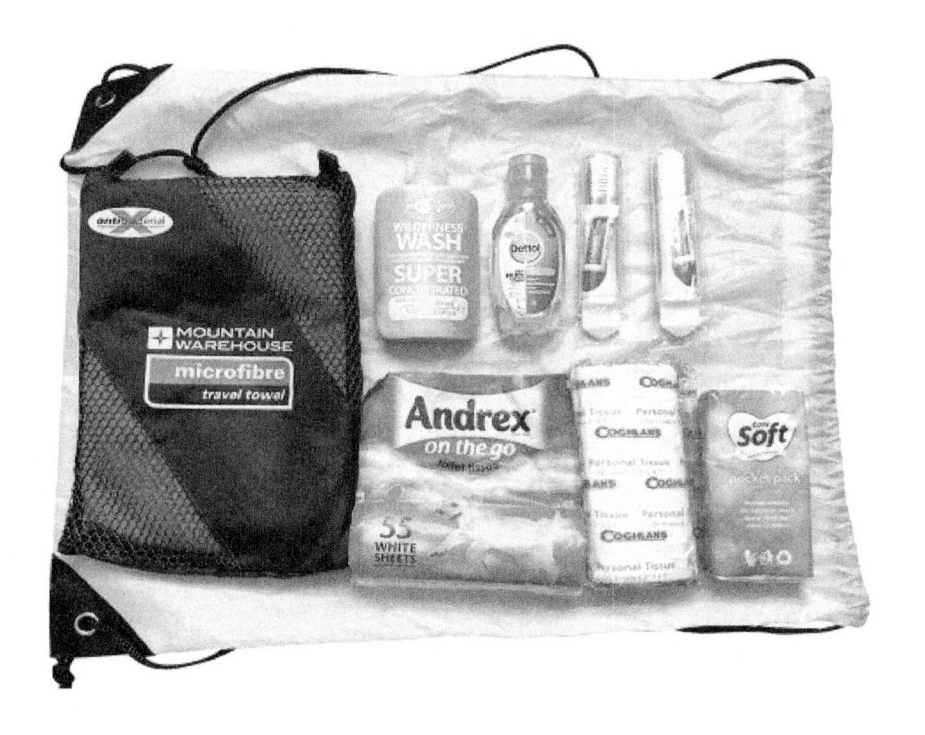

Get Home Bag or Secondary BUG OUT BAG

This bag is ideally a car version of your main bug out bag, or it is also ideal as a secondary person bag, i.e. Partner or Kids (teenager aged).
It's a very much smaller and far lighter bag, at least half the size and weight of your main bug out bag!

Commonly referred to as a Get Home Bag, the idea behind this bag is that it has everything needed to "get you home" for instance, if your vehicle gets stranded miles from anywhere and there is no phone signal, or if disaster strikes whilst you are at work, and you need to get home to your family but are a day or two away. Or need to travel on foot if roads are blocked etc.

*My preference bag is **KARRIMOR hot crag 25lt** size rucsac (approx. GB £25) Whatever the manufacturers might claim, NO bag is ever fully watertight. ALWAYS fit an inner "Dry Sac," some type of inner waterproof bag. Belts and braces, as my grandpa used to say…. never a bad thing having a back-up, double bagged will protect your life-saving equipment!!!*

Shelter and Environmental Protection
Fire Starting Kit (cotton wool balls soaked in petroleum jelly) + Disposable Lighters
6 x Tea Light Candles
Emergency Space Blanket

Reusable Rain Poncho
Sleeping Bag
Insulated Camping Mat or self-inflating mattress
Small Camping Tarp: *Great multi-use item, ideal for helping build a simple shelter fast and making it watertight*
2 x Toothbrushes and toothpaste
Small Sewing kit
Hand Sanitiser
Wet Wipes and Pocket Tissues
Travel Toilet Paper Roll
6 x Surgical 3 Ply Face Masks
Tube of superglue
Bandanna (face mask/injury pad)
+ or, Shemagh scarf – *bigger than a bandana at approx. 40" square and very useful as a head wrap, scarf, carry pouch, even a crude water filter if necessary*

Food and Water
Water bottle
1lt Water
Fishing Line and hooks
Food Rations: *Emergency rations and Kendal Mint Cake bars, dried fruits, nuts, granola/museli bars*
Water Purification Filtering Straw
Water Purification Tablets
Drinks Pouch
Manual Tin Can Opener
Eating Utensils SPORK cutlery
Small hand cheese grater *(this can double up to grate dry but rotten wood, to make the best fire-starting tinder!)*

Communication and Navigation
LED Head Torch lamp *(+ spare batteries)*
Pocket LED Light *(+ spare batteries)*
Wind Up Torch
Survival Whistle

Marine Flares (OPTIONAL: *Check laws affecting use and purchase of marine flares*)
Compass
Writing Note Pad, Pen and Pencil + sharpener
Chemical Light Sticks – NATO Military Grade
Signal Mirror
Pair Binoculars

Miscellaneous

Cash
Clothes
Identification (photocopies)
Multitool
Paracord or Braided Rope length
2 x Straps
PVC Tape Roll
Cable Ties selection
Dry Bag and 2 strong bin bags
Pocket Survival Guide
Work Gloves
Pocket Chainsaw
5 x Wax Household Candles 5hr burn
Microfibre Travel Towel

Self-Defence / First Aid

Sam Split Roll (*This is a mouldable support for broken bones*)
30-minute fire mask (Smoke filter)
Knife Sharpening Stone
Knife (SEE INDEX 2 Re UK knife laws)
Axe and or, Machete

First Aid Kit: -

Bandages/Safety Pins/ Tourniquet / Eye Wash Drops/ Paracetamol / Bug Repellent / Antiseptic Cream
Anti-Diarrhoea / Deet Insect Bug Repellent
1 x Midges / Mosquito Head Net
Clear Eye Safety Wraparound Glasses Goggles
CPR face mask

CHAPTER 9

Step 6: Shelter and Fire-Starting, Including Bug Out Camping and Survival

Including an introduction to food preservation and some of the more advanced water collection methods

> **TOP TIP and KEY POINT** *Learn some bushcraft and practise, practise, practise...You need to fully use and test out all of your equipment, as well as your ability to use it. Not dis-similar to learning and trying out the changing of a spare wheel on a new car. Far less stressful to try it out first at a time and a location of your choosing, maybe home and dry on your own driveway, rather than waiting for that puncture on a quiet country road with no phone signal and absolutely no idea how to even change the wheel.*

Bug Out Camping and Survival

ALWAYS do a few Bug out bag trial days, where you "bug out" and build a woodland shelter build and practise fire starting, etc. with a wild camp out few days.

Practise makes perfect, after all...
Key skills to practice are simple shelter constructions, using your fire starters, cooking over an open fire, and water filtration. With these basics mastered, you can survive far easier and definitely far more comfortably.

- Time your journey. Is your Bug Out location pre-programmed into your SatNav? Do you have a physical backup map, in case SatNav or phones stop working?
- Look for and note down areas and locations with possible problem hot spots or danger points, i.e., Where could you get jammed with traffic? Alternative routes, have you planned any? If you need to abandon your vehicle, have you looked where along your route you could get to on foot and still be secure and safe? Consider burying some key cache equipment dumps along the route.
- How safe and isolated is your chosen bug out location? Is it a piece of land you own, maybe some private woodland which you purchased? How easy would it be to defend? Does it have water, a stream, maybe?
- Is the location secure and private enough to risk having a fire, or would the smoke give away your location?
- Do you need to build a shelter, or if it is your own land, it is far better to prepare a shelter in advance and buy some hidden food and supply caches? Whenever possible, it is a great practise to have a few hidden supply dumps; having all of your supplies in one location is not the best practise! However, as in this book, we are generally concentrating on home preps, so I will not go into advanced techniques in too much detail at this stage. I want you to have a general overview and awareness of other things to consider. As well as some knowledge on building a basic and waterproof shelter.

Simple Shelter Building

> **TOP TIPS**
> 1.   Use a tarp from your Bug Out Bag to help create your shelter and for extra weather protection. By far, the absolute simplest way to set up a very quick and dry shelter in an emergency. In my Bug Out Bag contents, I advise having a pack of sailmakers needles and twine, as super useful for making repairs to tough materials on tarps, rucksacs, etc.
> 2.   Run out of paracord? Use a Plastic Bottle Cutter to create strong cordage (Always old plastic bottles around! This cool gadget can turn them into super survival cordage. With a flame from your fire, you can melt the cordage after using it to create a super-strong bond i.e., Creating a wooden table from saplings, use plastic cordage and melt into a super-strong seal) See Bug Out Bag contents list.

My favourite shelters are the simple "Lean To" or "A-Frame" shelter types. Firstly, you need to choose a good spot for your shelter, which is dry and flat *(if it rains, you do not want a stream of rainwater entering your camp bed!)*, and avoid building right next to a body of water which could overspill in heavy rain/floods.

Have the wind on your back; this way, when you build a fire for warmth, you won't get the smoke blowing into your shelter. Not even in bad weather, so wind and rain....

> **TIP:** When you build a fire, position it about 3ft / 1metre from your shelter entrance. Create a horseshoe shape made from rocks or big logs; this will act as a solid back and will ensure the heat is directed mainly towards your shelter.

Finally, definitely do not build below any cliffs as danger from falling rocks or even dead tree limbs, which could fall on you in high winds.
You can build these in many ways, such as draping a tarp over the fallen tree to make a tent. I prefer to lie branches upright along the fallen tree to create my "tent" camping area, then prop debris of leaves, branches, and vegetation to act as your shelter wall. If it is windy or cold, use other debris to block off the sides too. Ensure you "clean" your camp area of leaves, etc., which could catch fire from your fire's sparks, etc.
Initially, think KISS (Keep it Simple Stupid) a useful term and mind-set for much about prepping and emergency survival.

Pros for the "Lean To" and "A-Frame" type shelters
Easy to camouflage
Good protection from the elements, even against snow during winter.
Adaptable to various situations
Can be made easily with a tarp or with just woodland debris such as leaves, moss, soil, and branches

Cons
You may discover you are sharing your shelter with bugs from any rotting logs
Will take some time to gather debris to block off the entrance

Below are some of my favourite, easy to construct, shelter types...

A "Lean To" Shelter
1. Use your paracord to lash (tie) a sturdy horizontal branch between two upright trees. Or better yet, rest a horizontal branch over two of the trees lower branches to achieve the same effect (Simpler, quicker, and saves you using up your valuable paracord)
2. Lean multiple branches upright across the horizontal pole.
3. Ideally, at this point, use your waterproof tarp across these upright branches to keep the rain out of your shelter.
4. Now cover with leaves, moss, even soil to help waterproof and insulate your shelter

You can also utilise a natural rock outcrop to create a shelter
The below example shows a great cosy and fast build lean-to type shelter!

With a few basic tools and some creativity, you will be amazed at what shelter styles are possible to quickly construct.

"A-FRAME" Shelters

Similar to Lean To shelters, but double-sided for added protection and insulation.
For more than two people, it is best to keep both ends raised.
If solo, angled construction may be preferred
It is easier to block up the entrance at night time too

Wig Wam type Shelters

More headroom, but a lot more work to construct and make watertight
Has benefit that a small fire can be built inside, it must allow the ventilation of the smoke through the space

Simple tarp. Shelters

Quick and very easy to set up using a simple tarpulin and some paracord. It can be used in a whole variety of ways.

TIP: Don't forget to create a comfy chair for yourself too!

Tarp or Blanket Chair
Also, the same principle to construct it using a coat, blanket or sleeping back, etc.

Having a comfortable seat in camp is essential for any extended time. Being able to recline back and have your back supported is so much nicer than sitting on a tree stump or leaning against a tree whilst sat on a cold, damp ground! Think of this design a bit like a chair version of a hammock.

To Construct: -
Gather 4 durable posts, strong, flexible saplings approx. 1.5" - 2" diameter work best.
You need 3 upright poles cut to approx. 7-8-foot length, and a 4-foot long base pole. The support back pole, you may want to sharpen the ground end with your axe into a point, so it beds firmly into the ground for excellent

stability. The tripod centre can be lashed firmly together with paracord, or you can use a metal tripod support.

Dependent on your height, weight, etc., you may need to vary these, i.e., kids will only need a scaled-down version. So for this, I am simply giving you a grown man example.
Now loop your tarp or blanket over the seat pole and using some paracord, lash it to the tripod centre.

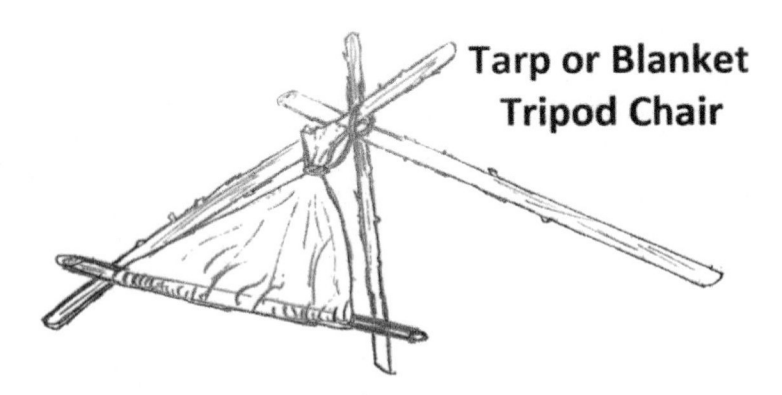

Tarp or Blanket Tripod Chair

FIRE STARTING Techniques

> *TOP TIPS*
> 1. Pre-soak some cotton wool balls in petroleum jelly "Vasoline," store in a secure plastic pouch; these make awesome fire starters! But high alcohol content hand sanitiser also is great to soak into your cotton wool balls before lighting. Silver birch tree bark is also a great natural tinder source.
> 2. Pack in your Bug Out Bag a small hand cheese grater; this can double up to grate dry but rotten wood to make the best ever fire-starting tinder powder!
> 3. Cotton Ear Buds (ideally card not plastic stems) and tampons can be pulled apart to make a surprisingly good amount of material for fire starting.

In basic terms, to make fire, you need just 3 elements: -
Oxygen, Fuel, and Heat

The greater the oxygen flow (i.e., blowing on a fire), the hotter the fire, and the faster it will burn your fuel. So consideration needs to be given as to what the fire is primarily for? Heat / Cooking or to provide slow, steady warmth throughout the night.

To start a fire, you need "tinder," tinder is a material that will easily ignite and first catch fire.
Part of your bug out kit will include matches/a lighter, and you definitely need a **magnesium flint fire striker**; see the below photo (these are weather and waterproof, and will last years). These create easy sparks in any weather and conditions. Personally, I favour a resin-based pinewood stick, or cotton wool balls pre-soaked in Vaseline (**Petrol**eum jelly...the clue is in the name). But high alcohol content hand sanitiser also is great to soak into your cotton wool balls before lighting. Silver birch tree bark is also a great natural tinder source

> *TIP: Carry a small hand cheese grater; this can double up to grate dry but rotten wood to make the best ever fire starting tinder!*

My preferred kit below can be found on below Amazon links: -
magnesium flint fire striker: https://amzn.to/2ZtRq24
I have mine attached to my tinder stick with some paracord
Pinewood, high resin content: https://amzn.to/3k6GXS2

First, gather 3 sizes of wood and create three piles in readiness for getting your fire going.

Start the fire using your tinder as above; then add very tiny twigs, dried grasses, and tree bark (silver birch tree bark is awesome to use), then add in your mid-sized twigs/branches, and once your file is well ablaze, you can add on the bigger logs.

Think pyramids and wigwam fire stacks; build your fire starting with your tiniest twigs and tinder on the inside first. You can even "feather" some small branches to help start the fire. Feathering is a technique using your knife to slice shavings all along the branch, leaving them still attached, though. These smaller wood "feathers" on the branch will ignite far easier as they are smaller yet with good surface area and good airflow around them.

Smaller sized fires are often best because they are sufficient for heat and for cooking, whilst being small enough to be easily controlled. Plus, they will take longer to use up your gathered wood supply. Time and energy expanded always should be key survival awareness in all your activities.

WARNING
Ensure you control your fire. Fires can quickly turn very dangerous and out of control. *(Special awareness on peat soils, once peat burns, it can burn out of control even underground and is almost impossible to put out without an awful lot of water!)*
Rock around a fire is the classic safety measure. Some people favour more of a contained dug fire pit style where you first dig down so that the fire is slightly below ground level.
If your fire gets out of control, smother it as quickly and safely as possible. Water, soil, etc. anything to stop the oxygen, reaching it.
If your clothing catches fire, drop to the ground, cover your face with your hands, and roll until the flames are out. Obviously, water, a towel (ideally wet), or even soil will work. Again, the idea is to simply cut off the oxygen supply.
Any burns need very careful treatment; this should always be learned as to be part of your First Aid training

TIPS:
- Clean any debris from all around your fire; you do not want sparks setting alight your camp!
- Build a horseshoe shape around the back of the fire. Not only to contain the fire but with a raised back wall, your fire will reflect the heat towards you and be far more efficient.
A simple branch wall works great, ideally use green saplings as these are full of moisture and less likely to become hot enough to catch fire. Simply hammer in four upright branches about 3-4 ft. tall, then infill with horizontal sapling branches. This "wall" will direct the heat from the fire towards your camp bed and is surprisingly effective. If you have the time and energy, make 2 smaller side "walls" and create a horseshow around the back of the fire.

- Wet ground? Start with a layer of dry or dryish logs and build your fire on top of that platform. If all your wood is wet, use your knife to shave off the top layers till you reach dryer wood.
- Another great tip for starting a fire with wet wood is to split it down the centre, the middle part will still be dry. Feather it / shave some out of the centre for great dry tinder.
- Aim for dry, not living green wood as this is full of moisture. Dry wood will "crackle" when snapped in half, green wood will not, plus green wood fires will usually be a lot less hot and far more smokey. (not great if your aim is to be camping more covertly; the hotter the fire, the less it smokes)
- If there is a lack of smaller twigs or wood bark, etc., use your knife to "feather" small shavings off the log, which will catch fire easier
- Lack of a wood source? Try dried animal dung, or even dead animals themselves, as any fat left on the carcass will greatly aid the firing process

Dakota Fire Pit: one of my very favourite and more covert low smoke fire options!

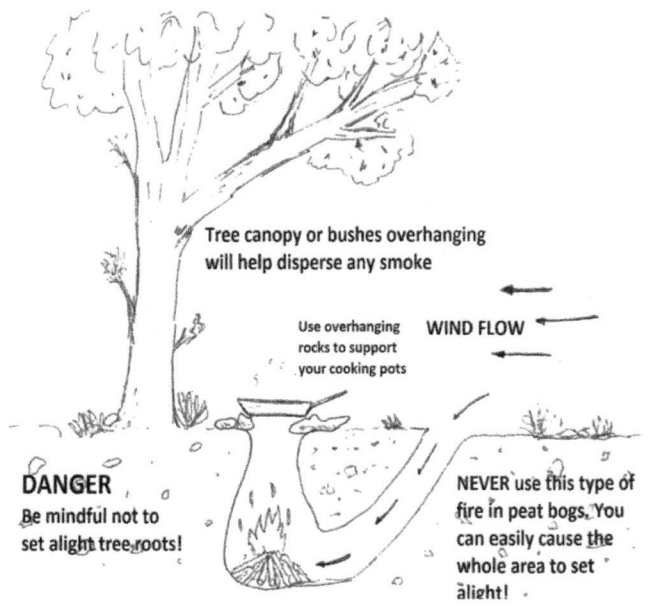

Tree canopy or bushes overhanging will help disperse any smoke

Use overhanging rocks to support your cooking pots

WIND FLOW

DANGER Be mindful not to set alight tree roots!

NEVER use this type of fire in peat bogs. You can easily cause the whole area to set alight!

The Dakota Fire Pit, named after the Native American tribe of the Dakota. The key advantage of this style of fire is to combat the local windy conditions; plus, it greatly lessens the danger of accidentally starting grass bush fires. The fire can be made deeper for cooking over or shallower for just generating heat.

This technique is still popular to this day, particularly so with us preppers. The airflow generated through the pit creates a super-efficient heat source. Oxygen is channelled directly to the fire and uses up far less wood than many other fire options. There is also the added benefit of an easy to manage the cooking area.

For preppers, while the reduced wood usage is important, the fact that the fire being mainly below ground is a big advantage when trying to remain undetected. The benefit of the hot clean burning process is that it greatly reduces smoke, thus making it easier to remain less visible from a distance. Any smoke present can be further reduced if the fire pit is located near overhanging trees or bushes; the foliage can further disperse and filter any smoke created.

It is, however, time-consuming to build and requires suitable ground soil and conditions to be easily dug. This makes it practical only if you plan to be staying in the same location for more than a day or two.

WARNING: never use this fire type in areas of peat ground; these fires generate a lot of heat and can easily set fire to tree roots; a whole tree can easily fully burn from the inside out if the fire has started in their root system. Also, if peat ground, the high heat generated can actually set alight the whole ground area and are then next to impossible to put out!

Two favourite fires of mine :

1. Swedish Log Fire

Regular ones are 10"–14" size but can be sunk into the ground for stability and can be made as a huge dramatic version...these look stunning.

Also called a Swedish Torch, Canadian Candle and in Finland, it is called the Raappanan tuli candle
This type of fire method, in some form, has been used by woodsmen dating right back to the medieval period.

The Schwedenfackel, or fire torch in Swedish, its name is believed to originate during the 30 Year War, which started in1618 and during the war when firewood was scarce, so soldiers were looking for a way to conserve their wood. That was about 400 years ago. What worked then still works now.

This is a great fire for heat and cooking. Simple to make and log lasting.
Find a log approx. 10-20" long. Using your axe, split the log into quarters. (There is a lazy chainsaw method. Same principle but keeping the whole log, chainsaw down 75% of its length to keep its shape and stability. Making it ideal for using far taller logs and burying them in the ground, little way to stop them toppling over)

A good tip is to mark each quarter 1,2,3,4,5,6 with a pen or make some kind of distinguishing mark with your knife. This will help when you put it back in the right order! It's useful to have some wire to hold the sections in place. Most preppers will have some wire with them as it's a popular material for making animal snares from.

Using your axe, "feather the logs" (see photo below) down their length to catch alight and burn better (The same principle to feathering kindling when starting a fire. When you reassemble the log, the feathered tips should point downwards for the best angle to take light.
Fill the gaps, sides, etc. with small twigs, wood shavings, tree bark, etc. and set it alight. You will first see a lot of smoke leaving the chimney, blow in the gaps to help get it going with the extra oxygen. Once the inside is lit, and the feathers continue to burn, you'll start to see flames shoot out of the top.

It is often advisable to leave it going for about 15 minutes; then, it is easier to add a metal stove topper, or place rocks on top or a hammer in series of nails, to support the cooking pan. Raising your cooking pan is simply to allow better airflow and generate a hotter heat.

The Lazy Person Swedish Log Stove

Pretty much the same effect can be created by using some wire to lash together 3 medium-sized logs, feather and chip away the inner facing sides to help them catch fire better (see above photo). Fill the centre hole with tinder and set it alight!

The wire will simply hold it all together…No wire? Simply gather longer branches and bury the ends approx. 6" in the ground for stability or surround the log trio with rocks to achieve the same result, stability.

Nice, quick, and easy fire stove.

The Lazy Swedish Log Stove

Rocket Log Stove Fire - Log Candle Torch

In my opinion, these are the coolest ever fires and will burn for hours and hours!

It's as simple as just drilling two holes. I like to use the manual Scotch Handle Auger 1 - 1.5" drill, which is 8-10" long, easy to carry in your pack, and you create the handle from an old branch found lying around your camp.

Image courtesy of CORPORALS CORNER

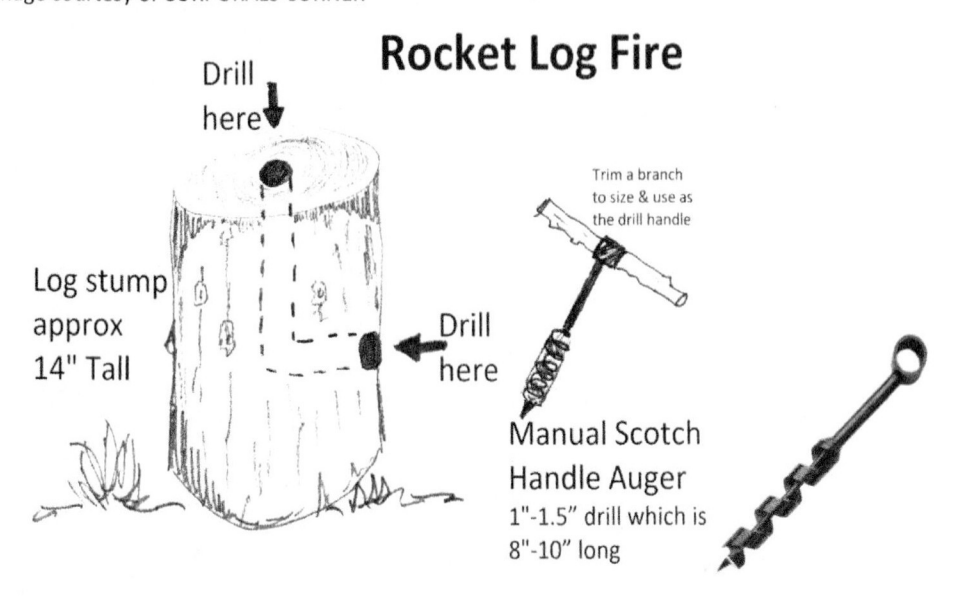

Rocket Log Fire

Drill here

Log stump approx 14" Tall

Drill here

Trim a branch to size & use as the drill handle

Manual Scotch Handle Auger
1"-1.5" drill which is 8"-10" long

The holes need to line up, creating a letter "L" shape. Then, clean out some of the sawdust to allow a clear airflow. Next, start your fire with a few twigs and some of the removed sawdust. Once the fire gets going, there is no need to add extra wood as the stove itself becomes the fuel for the fire burning from the inside out.

HOW TO TRAP and CATCH ANIMALS, then onto how to preserve the meat
Interesting fact, the flesh of ALL furred mammals and birds is edible

Some great tutorial web sites are:
https://therealsurvivalists.com/traps-and-snares/

https://www.offgridweb.com/survival/6-trap-triggers-for-survival/

https://www.gutenberg.org/files/34110/34110-h/34110-h.htm

SIMPLE SNARES AND TRAPS
The below images are from my Bug Out Bag; these are my rabbit/squirrel snares

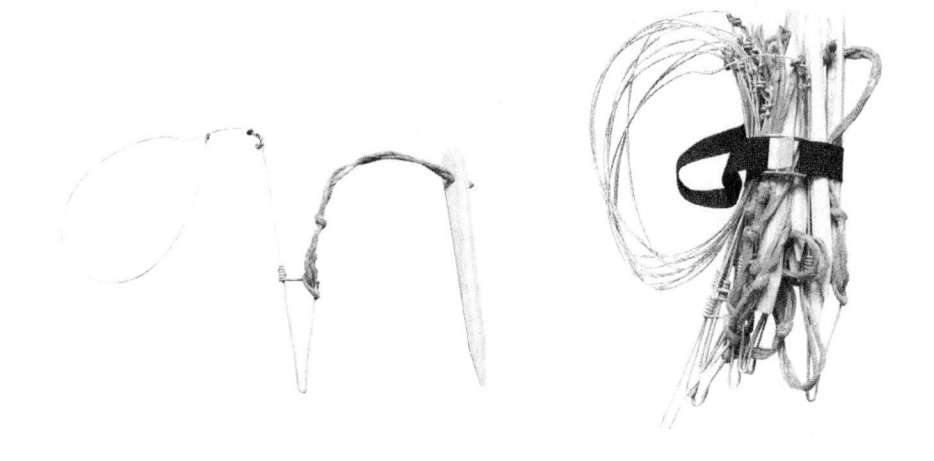

In simple terms, a snare is a loop, usually brass or metal cable, but can be paracord too. This loop will tighten, ideally around an animal's neck, but can be a limb. Wire is far better than rope or your paracord, as animals cannot chew it.

In principal, I am not a fan of snares as they can cause much pain and distress to the captured animal. We have all heard of stories of animals gnawing off its own foot to escape. However, in times of survival, you need to be aware of all options in order to catch your food.

SNARING BEST PRACTICES
Unless a genuine survival situation, some snares, and traps can actually be illegal.
It is vital that snares are checked at least daily to prevent undue suffering to any trapped animals, but **ideally checked every 4-8 hours**

1. Funnelling: Using branches, rocks, and logs, create a funnel that forces your animal into your trap. If you can't bait your trap, funnelling draws an animal into the snare that it would otherwise try to avoid.

2. Multiple Traps: Trap works best on the principle of the more, the better. A single snare covering a rabbit hole may pay off, but multiple overlapping snares will increase your odds. The same concept goes for crushing traps — On average, only one out of 20 traps set will catch anything, so make sure they're easy and energy effective to set up.

3. Watch Your Eyes and Fingers: Whenever you're setting a trap, there's a possibility you'll accidentally trigger it. Eye injuries and crushed fingers are the most common type of injuries. Respect your traps and what damage they can do.

4. Check Frequently: Traps can be triggered inadvertently, and a trap that isn't set won't catch anything. Traps can be blown over by the wind, or they might just injure an animal, allowing it to possibly escape before you return. Traps should be checked every four to eight hours.

5. Dispatch Safely: Ideally, snares will wrap a loop around an animal's neck and either snap the spine or strangle it. Sadly, snares can sometimes catch an animal around the head and shoulder, around the body, or around one or both of the rear legs. If you catch an animal that's still squirming in a trap, you need a way to dispatch it quickly and humanely. A good forked stick will help pin it down or against a tree. A hard strike to the head with a branch will do the rest.

6. Reset Traps: Animals are creatures of habit, and the instincts that attracted your first animal to the snare trap you set may well lead others there too. If your trap isn't damaged from the first kill, reset it and check it later.

7. Baiting Traps: Baiting traps will improve your odds hugely. Scavenged mushrooms, berries, nuts, and animal guts can be harvested in the wild, depending on the usual diet of the animal you're trying to trap.

Common Snare Types

Traps and Snares – Mainly 4 types: Strangle, Tangle, Dangle or Mangle

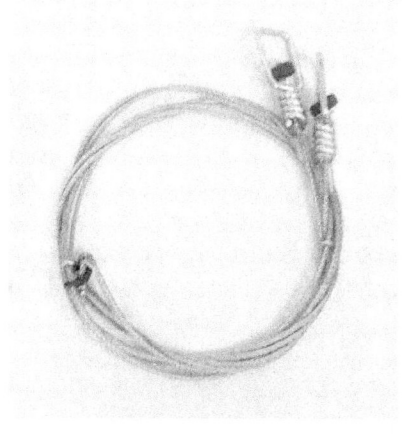

Galvanised wire snare example

1. **Strangle type** (also known as a Poachers Knot)
   In basic terms, a loop needs to be positioned ideally at head height (animal head, i.e., rabbit, fox, deer, etc.) with a wire firmly secured to

a tree or stake firmly driven in the ground. Ideally positioned over an animal's den hole entrance. The loop needs to be at the animal's head height. Once caught, the struggling animal will tighten the noose and strangle itself.

As per the photo, I prefer using rabbit snares with a wire tealer as they are thinner so less visible even though they are longer. Also, they are stronger and set more firmly fixed in the ground, keeping the snare far better in position. They help hold the snare loop at the right height so that it catches the animal's head correctly (approx. 6" above ground) and will hold the snare loop correctly across the animals run so that it is square to the direction of travel.
Because they form an integral part of the snare, being anchored to the peg at one end and the snare at the other, the wire tealer forms a natural swivel and greatly reduces the chances of a rabbit becoming tangled.

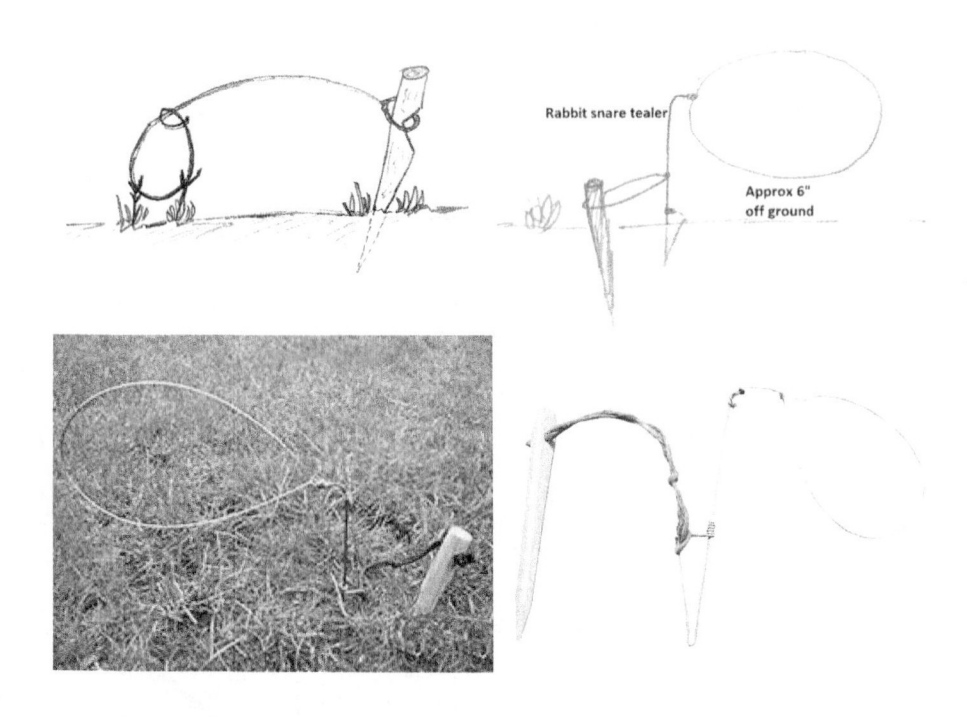

Rabbit snare tealer

Approx 6" off ground

Multiple Trap Snare

Infill gaps to funnel prey into noose

Adjust noose height in line with size of bird/animal you are trying to snare

2. **Dangle type**- Spring Tension Snares
   Not dissimilar to the above but adapted with the use of a strong and springy sapling branch.
   The advantage with this snare is that the prey is raised off the ground and less likely to become a free meal to another passing animal!
   It is "triggered" when the struggling animal dislodges the notched wood, and the bent sapling swings back to its usual upright position taking the captured animal with it.

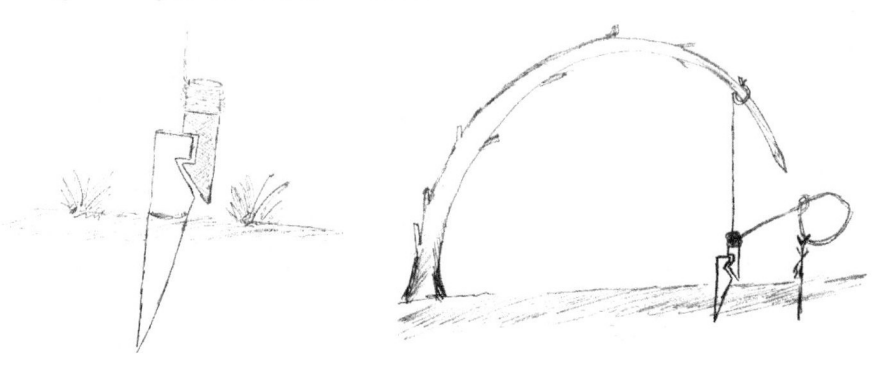

Alternative style of a Spring Snare
Held in place by two hammered into the ground and notched sticks, with horizontal trigger stick.
Held under tension by a bent-over spaling.

Position rocks and bushes either side to force the prey to pass into your noose. The bait hanging from the horizontal trigger will attract your prey further forward.

Spring Snare

Attach paracord to a bent over sapling

3. **Tangle type** – Tree / "Noose" Snares
   SQUIRREL POLE SNARE
   In effect, simply lean a long branch against a tree, thus creating an easier route up and into the tree for the animal. Along the branch, position several snares to catch the animal that runs along the branch on its way into the tree. Wrap the snare around the tree and position the snare loop on top of the branch/pole, so the animal runs straight into it. However, it is important that the trap has a knot and starts under the branch of the tree; only the noose is positioned at the top. The reason is that when the squirrel gets caught, it will try to leap clear, and will fall off left hanging below the branch. They will hang ready for collection on your regular inspection visits; they will often attract other squirrels who also could get snared, so not uncommon to catch a few with this one trap method.
   This snare works the best with squirrels as they are neophiliacs, a love of or enthusiasm for what is new or novel. It can also be used to catch small birds when positioned on a horizontal tree branch.
   A newly positioned log in their woods will prove irresistible for squirrels to explore.

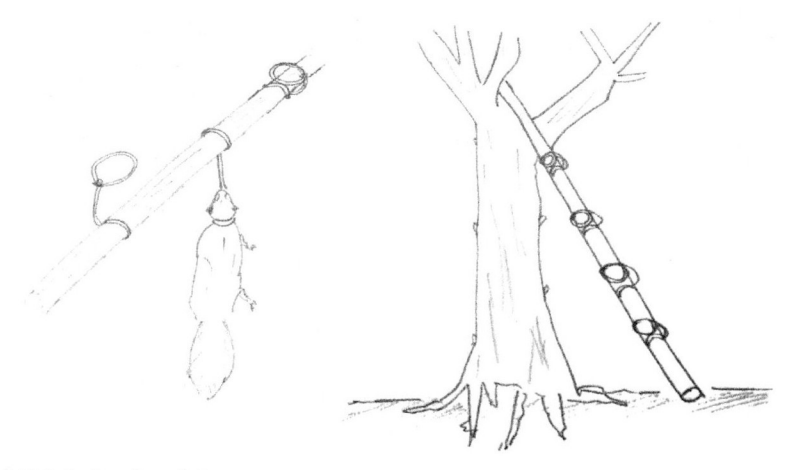

Forked Stick Squirrel Snare
Another popular version of the squirrel snare uses a forked stick; this helps with positioning and is more accurate to entice the squirrel to go exactly where you want…. directly into the noose! But it does take longer to set your snares.

Forked Stick Squirrel Snare

4. **Tangle type** – Leg / Trap Floor Spring Snare.
   The trap floor snare is both simple and effective, suitable for catching prey of all sizes. Bend over a springy sapling and tension in place by a length of paracord. Hide the wire loop with leaves to help disguise it. Squirrels, rabbits, etc. are easily snared; even bigger prey such as deer can be caught using a larger version of this method.
   Push two sticks tied together into the ground. Attach a length of paracord from a bent over, under tension sapling is tied to your

wooden toggle, and the toggle passed under the baited line. When the game takes the bait, it releases the toggle that flies up, taking the snare and the game with it.

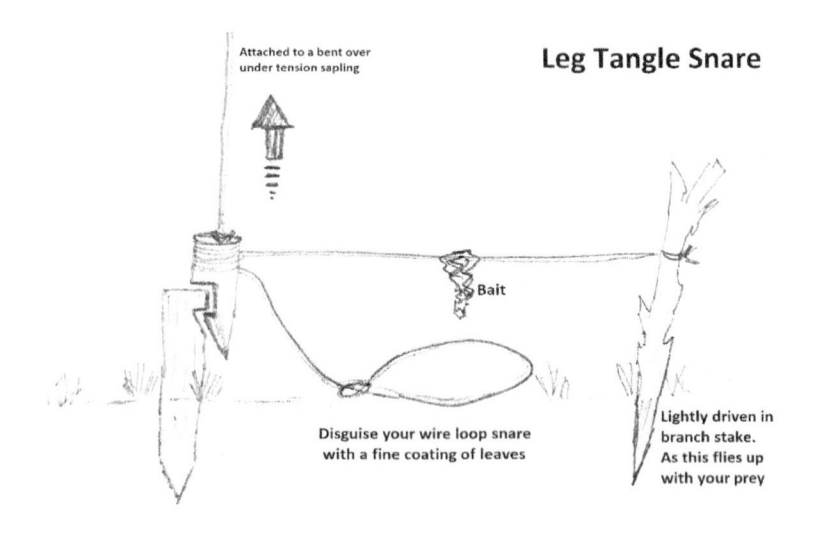

Leg Tangle Snare

Attached to a bent over under tension sapling

Bait

Disguise your wire loop snare with a fine coating of leaves

Lightly driven in branch stake. As this flies up with your prey

5. **Mangle type** – a DEADFALL figure 4 trigger
   Quite a time-consuming trap to set up. This can be a difficult snare to set up. Often referred to as a figure 4 trigger.
   This snare needs 3 sticks of different sizes, constructed to form a number 4 shape.
   A horizontal bait bar is balanced at right angles to an upright with a lock bar, which supports a rock or other heavyweight pivoting around the tip of the upright. The animal will approach to take a bite of the bait and thus dislodge the trigger. A large log or stone will fall onto their head or body. The best set triggers are the most sensitive you can make them, but these are also the hardest to set and the easiest to be triggered by the wind and not the desired animal.

Figure 4
DEADfall Snare

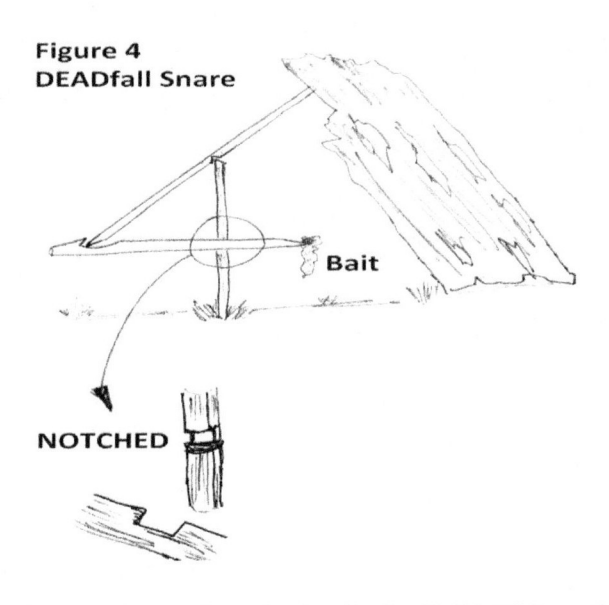

Bait

NOTCHED

6. **A simpler and more favourite of mine is the Split Stick or Split Fork Deadlift design**
   Very sensitive and light trigger, you also need to watch you do not crush your own hand in setting this trap up!
   Simple two-piece trigger, once your prey goes for the bail, it dislodges the balanced branch and the rest comes down to gravity.

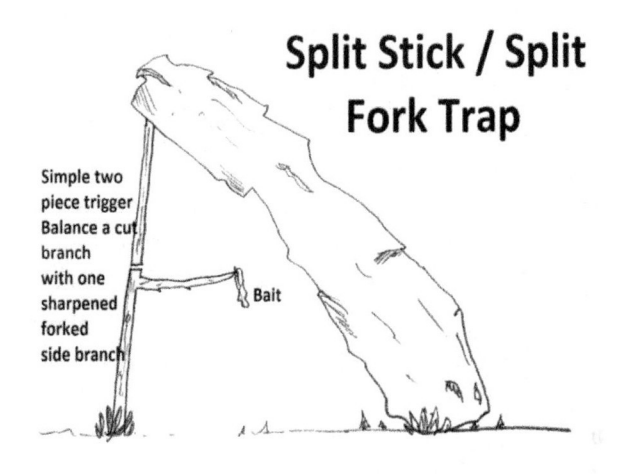

Split Stick / Split Fork Trap

Simple two piece trigger
Balance a cut branch with one sharpened forked side branch

Bait

7. **Portable Snare –**

    Great for taking a quick and easy snare to set up with you. This design uses only 3 re-usable shaped wood and some paracord with a wire loop.

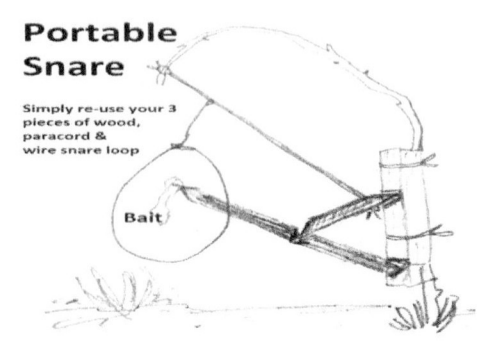

    Portable Snare

    Simply re-use your 3 pieces of wood, paracord & wire snare loop

    Bait

8. **DEADLY Pitfall –**

    A firm TV favourite! Easiest of all traps, simply dig a hole in the patch of an animal run, cover lightly with leaves and thin sticks. Ideally, place some tempting "bait" in the centre. If you want a more deadly trap, place sharpened sticks pointing upwards in the bottom of the pit. **BUT always leave signs to clearly warn hikers about the position of the traps!!!**
    Large pits could be used to catch bigger game such as boar or deer.

9. **Classic Pitfall Traps -**

    These come in a variety of sizes and designs. Two main forms: dry and wet pitfall traps.

    The opening is usually covered by a sloped stone or lid or some other such object. This is to reduce the amount of rain and debris falling into your trap, and to prevent animals in dry traps from drowning (when it rains) or even from overheating (during the day) as well as to keep out predators.

A. Dry pitfall traps are basically just a bucket or other such container buried in the ground with its rim at surface level. These will trap animals that fall into them.

B. Wet pitfall traps are basically the same, but contain a solution designed to kill and preserve the trapped animals. The fluids that can be used in these traps include formalin (10% formaldehyde), methylated spirits, alcohol, ethylene glycol, trisodium phosphate, picric acid, or even (with daily checked traps) plain water. A little detergent is usually added to break the surface tension of the liquid to promote quicker more humane drowning.

Some sort of funnelling may be added to channel your prey into the trap. Branches and rocks etc. piled either side, for instance.
Traps may also be baited to increase the chance of success placing them in, above, or near the trap. Examples of baits include meat, dung, fruit, and pheromones.

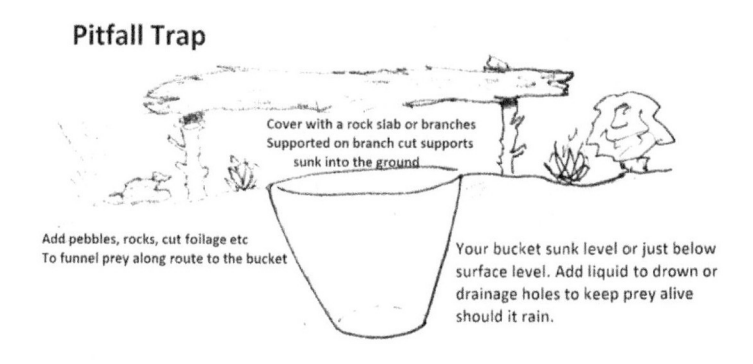

Pitfall Trap

Cover with a rock slab or branches Supported on branch cut supports sunk into the ground

Add pebbles, rocks, cut foilage etc To funnel prey along route to the bucket

Your bucket sunk level or just below surface level. Add liquid to drown or drainage holes to keep prey alive should it rain.

10. Triangle Bird Snare / Coat hanger snare

The idea is to hang it within the branches of a tree to trap smaller sized birds.
A bird will land on the lower horizontal branch, this falls away, and your wire snare loo will trap the bird.
Using paracord, tie two small sticks together (or use one forked stick), insert between the cord a small sharpened stick to hold the bait. Finally, loosely position a smaller horizontal" perch" stick for the bird to land on, but ensure this is very lightly in place as it needs to fall

away the moment the bird lands on it. The perch stick will drop away, and the bird will get caught in the noose wire.

TIP: Works best with 2 wire snares either side as traps success depends on the bird flying in over wire snare direction!

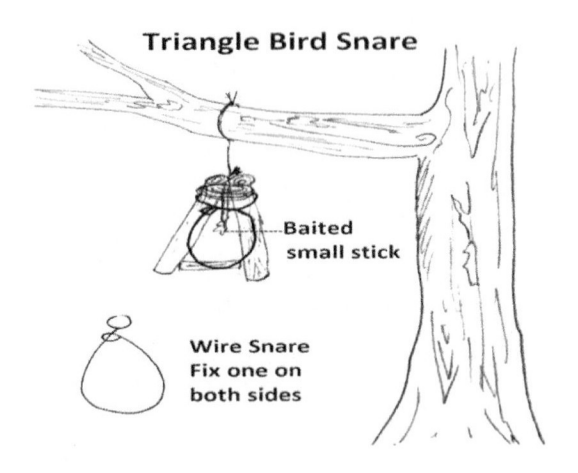

Triangle Bird Snare

Baited small stick

Wire Snare
Fix one on both sides

11. Bird Snare – Living Prey Trap

BIRD Snare, or as a way to keep animal prey "fresh" until you get back to check your snare. Based on a Figure 4 snare assembly, but with a basket, not Deadfall drop.

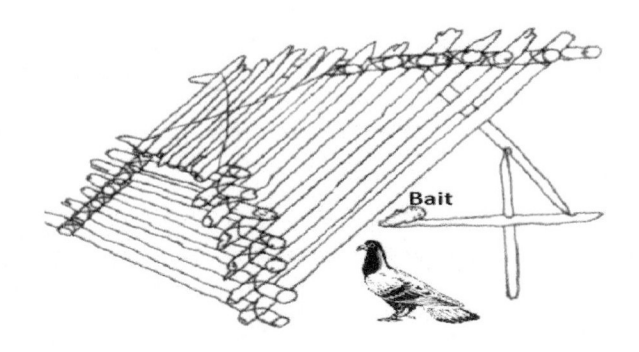

Figure 4 Bird Trap

Bait

12. Fishing Spring Snare –

Just a variation on a traditional classic bent sapling spring snare, with the simple addition of a float and fishing hook (ideally baited with a worm or bug).

When the fish takes the bait, it dislodges the notched stick and releases the bent sapling tree

Simple, but very effective.

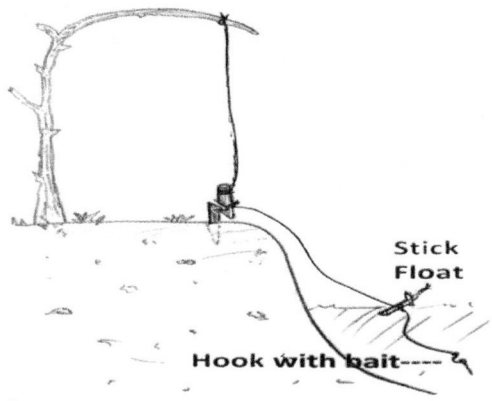

BUTCHERING your snared prey
TIPS re knives etc.
- Use some type of food-grad oil on your knives and equipment if you also intend to use them to prepare your food. The oil protects against rust, and using food-grade means that you do not run the risk of swallowing toxic oils.
- In the field, you will need at least a sharpening stone, as processing your meat requires very sharp edges.
- When butchering an animal, use the anatomical lines to guide your knife, do not just try to cut through them. Cut between bones and at joint points rather than trying to chop through them.
- Do not throw away anything; whatever you do not use, can be used as bait in your snares and traps.
- In a survival situation, it is vital to do everything you can to avoid getting sick. When dealing with raw meat preparation, avoid cross-contamination, and always wash everything thoroughly before using them on another process.

HANGING meats

A quick comment on hanging your prey. So many people imagine it will go off and start to smell. However, the aim is actually to allow the meat to relax and to concentrate its flavours.

HOWEVER, there seems to be no hard and fast room with hanging game meat. Some suggest eating rabbits right away, some advice between 2-7 days. But here's a rough guide on hanging times (*weather dependent, hang away from other predators and try to keep flies off it*) Hang at a temperature of 5°C, though this should be shortened if the temperature is warmer. Meanwhile, food safety experts say that pheasant should be hung for no longer than a week, ideally for three days at 4°C.

Hanging your birds by the neck or feet does not matter; there is no difference with either method, and is a simple matter of tying them and popping them up on a hook, feathers and guts still intact

Rabbits – 1-7 days
Pheasants – 3-5 days
Partridges – 2-3 days

My favourite book on this subject is Mike Robinsons "Fit for Table" ISBN 978-1-84689-006-2

I attended The Mike Robinson "Game and Wild Food Cookery School" in Berkshire, UK, back in 2014. A very informative, hands-on, and really enjoyable days' course. Highly recommended.

SMALL MAMMALS: i.e. Rabbits and Squirrels
Remove the head and limbs, then gut the animal. Small animals like rabbit and squirrel can be skinned without the need to hang them. Use your knife to cut along the backbone and peel away the skin and fur.

LARGE MAMMALS: i.e. Deer and Wild Boar
As soon as the animal is dead, wearing gloves, turn the animal on its side, with your knife, cut deep around the anus (on a doe, around the vulva), pull all this out, and tie it off so as not to contaminate your meat.
Next, gut the animal, taking great care not to perforate the lower organs with your knife.
Now, roll the animal onto its back, with its rear end ideally facing slightly downhill. Insert your knife directly below the breastbone, use an angle towards the neck to avoid puncturing the stomach. All you are doing is opening up an air gap in the body cavity.
Carefully form your fingers into a "V" and, with your knife, cut all the way down to the pelvis.
You can now remove the external male organs as well as removing its internal organs, cutting away any connective tissue from the body cavity. Then hang the body, ready for processing and cutting up.

SMALL GAME BIRDS:
To easily reach the usable breast meat, put the bird closely between your feet whilst standing on its wings. Life up from its fit, and this will separate the carcass and expose the bird's breast flesh.

LARGER GAME BIRDS: i.e., Duck, Turkey, Pheasant
Plucking procedure
Grasp the bird by its feet, and wingtip ends together. Starting from the base of the breast, grasp the feathers firmly between thumb and forefinger. Push your hand forward in short, rapid movements. Do not grasp too many feathers at once, or you will pull the skin off with the feathers. Always pluck against the lie of the feathers.

Turn the bird over and repeat on the sides and underneath of the wings. Remove the wings at the pivot joint with a cleaver, or knife. Next, remove the tail, remove the legs at the knee joint and also remove the head.
TIP: any downy soft under feathers remaining can easily be burnt off by carefully rotating over your campfire.

Start by plucking the feathers as above. Lay the bird on its back and cut just below the breast bone and slice (or tear with your fingers) all the way down to the anus. With the sides of your hands, push the skin down and away from the breasts. Finally, with a sharp boning knife, you can remove the fleshy breast meat.

Recipe examples for your snared prey
Look online for lots of variations on snares, traps along with recipe ideas for how best to cook and enjoy your prey. Here are a few great ones to get you started!

RABBIT Stew: *works equally with pheasant/squirrel etc. too*
1 large rabbit, skinned and gutted, then cut up into 8 pieces
6 pieces of chopped up bacon
4 large carrots, cut into chunks
8 potatoes, quartered
2 cloves crushed garlic
½ cup of apple cider vinegar
1 medium onion, diced
2 tablespoons butter
3 tablespoons all-purpose flour
2 teaspoons salt
2 teaspoons ground pepper
Place rabbit pieces in a cast iron pot and cover with water. Put on a campfire and bring to boil, boil for a further 5 minutes. Add rest of ingredients, top-up water till everything just covered.
Slow cook over medium heat for 1 – 1.5 hours.

RABBIT Confit with Garlic and Rosemary

4 large rabbit, skinned and gutted, then cut up into legs, shoulders, and the saddle cut in two
NB. Make sure to remove the livers, belly flap, ribs, and pelvis.
Plain Flour for dusting
1lt Olive Oil (not extra virgin Olive oil as its flavour is too strong)
1lt White Wine
5 Bulbs (whole bulbs) Garlic, cut in half across the middle
20 sprigs of Rosemary
2 teaspoons salt
2 teaspoons ground pepper
1 Lemon for squeezing on meal

Start by heating a small amount of olive oil in a pan. Dip each joint of the rabbit in your flour. Fry the rabbit joints a few at a time for colouring, then transfer to a large Dutch Oven (Cast iron Casserole dish in other words)
Pour over the olive oil, wine and add the garlic bulbs (skins left on) and the Rosemary sprigs. Stir in.
Place a layer of greaseproof paper onto the top of the liquid (do not use pan lid as we want the liquid to be able to reduce down a bit).
Cook for 2 to 3 hours over low heat. Stir occasionally and check the rabbit flesh hasn't got stuck to the bottom of your pan.

When ready, squeeze over the lemon juice and serve immediately. The meat should be super tender and fall off the bone.

FRIED POTATOES WITH SQUIRREL:

TIP: Boil the squirrel the night before. The meat is ready when it is at the falling off the bone stage. Drain water and remove all the bones. Store meat in a cool place, away from hungry beasties.
1 Squirrel, skinned and gutted
½ teaspoon garlic powder
2 medium potatoes
1 medium onion
Lard, for pan-frying

Boil squirrel in a pot. Shred the meat and add in some garlic powder. Grease a frying pan with lard, heat over low heat. Dice the onion, peel and slice the potatoes, add the squirrel meat and fry everything on a medium/high heat until the potatoes are golden brown.

JAM GLAZED PHEASANT:
2 pheasants
¼ cup of salt
1 jar raspberry jam
½ cup of water

Remove feathers, rinse, remove giblets and pat dry.
Sprinkle cavity with salt, tie legs together and cook for 1.5 – 2 hours until meat is tender.
Mix water and jam in a pan and bring to the boil, baste the pheasants frequently with the mixture.
Serve with wild rice and mix in any remaining jam mixture.

Preserving the food you have caught/trapped.

For advanced prepping, it will be important for you to acquire knowledge on how to preserve any meat or fish which you may have caught. Food may be hard to come by and needs to be carefully treated and rationed. Food "spoils" very quickly indeed without the modern-day comforts of fridges and freezers. Rancid food will make you seriously ill, and in a survival situation, this could spell disaster. If you learn how to preserve food, you will have a precious resource that can sustain you for months.

It is worth noting, however, that some methods of food preservation are known to create carcinogens. In 2015, the International Agency for Research on Cancer of the World Health Organization classified processed meat, i.e., meat that has undergone salting, curing, fermenting, and smoking, as "carcinogenic to humans. But if you're in a survival situation, you need to use what is available to you.

The full list of traditional ways of preserving food includes: -
FOR FULL INFO, See
https://en.wikipedia.org/wiki/Food_preservation#Curing

1. **Curing**: Dehydration or drying techniques were used as early as 12,000 BC.

2. **Cooling and Freezing**: Great for our modern lives, not so easy during survival times

3. **Boiling**: Boiling liquid food items can kill any existing microbes. Milk and water are often boiled to kill any harmful microbes that may be in them.

4. **Heating**: Heating to temperatures which are sufficient to kill microorganisms inside the food. This is the method used to keep perpetual stews safe! Milk is also boiled before storing to kill many microorganisms.

5. **Sugaring**: Sugaring can be used in the production of jam and jelly. Preserves are made by heating the fruit with sugar. The sugar draws water from the microbes (plasmolysis) and leaves the microbial cells dehydrated, thus killing them.

6. **Pickling**: The food is placed in an edible liquid that inhibits or kills bacteria and other microorganisms. Typical pickling agents include brine (high in salt), vinegar, alcohol, and vegetable oil. Many chemical pickling processes also involve heating or boiling so that the food being preserved becomes saturated with the pickling agent.

7. **Lye**: Sodium hydroxide (lye) makes food too alkaline for bacterial growth. Lye will saponify fats in the food, which will change its flavour and texture. Lutefisk uses lye in its preparation, as do some olive recipes. Modern recipes for century eggs also call for lye.

8. **Canning**: See page 130

9. **Jellying**: Food may be preserved by cooking in a material that solidifies to form a gel. Such materials include gelatine, agar, maize flour, and arrowroot flour. Some foods naturally form a protein gel when cooked, such as eels. Besides jellying of meat and seafood, a widely known type of Jellying is fruit preserves, which are preparations of fruits, vegetables, and sugar, often stored in glass jam jars and Mason jars. Many varieties of fruit preserves are made globally, including sweet fruit preserves, such as those made from strawberry or apricot, and savoury preserves, such as those made from tomatoes or squash. The ingredients used and how they are prepared to determine the type of preserves; jams, jellies, and marmalades are all examples of different styles of fruit preserves that vary based upon the fruit used. In English, the word "preserves" is used to describe all types of jams and jellies.

10. **Jugging**: Meat can be preserved by jugging. Jugging is the process of stewing the meat (commonly game or fish) in a covered earthenware jug or casserole. The animal to be jugged is usually cut into pieces, placed into a tightly-sealed jug with brine or gravy, and stewed. Red wine and/or the animal's own blood is sometimes added to the cooking liquid. Jugging was a popular method of preserving meat up until the middle of the 20th century.

11. **Burial**: Burial of food can preserve it due to a variety of factors: lack of light, lack of oxygen, cool temperatures, pH level, or desiccants in the soil. Burial may be combined with other methods such as salting or fermentation. Most foods can be preserved in soil that is very dry and salty (thus a desiccant) such as sand, or soil that is frozen.

Many root vegetables are very resistant to spoilage and require no other preservation than storage in cool dark conditions (see ROOT CELLARS page 134), for example, by burial in the ground, such as in a storage clamp. Sometimes meat is buried under conditions that cause preservation. If buried on hot coals or ashes, the heat can kill pathogens, the dry ash can desiccate, and the earth can block oxygen and further contamination. If buried where the earth is very cold, the earth acts like a refrigerator.

Butter and similar substances have been preserved as bog butter in Irish peat bogs for centuries.

12   **Confit**: Meat can be preserved by salting it, cooking it at or near 100 °C in some kind of fat (such as lard or tallow), and then storing it immersed in the fat. These preparations were popular in Europe before refrigerators became ubiquitous. They are still popular in France, where they are called confit. The preparation will keep longer if stored in a cold cellar or buried in a cold ground.

13.   **Fermentation**: Some foods, such as many cheese, wines, and beers, use specific micro-organisms that combat spoilage from other less-benign organisms. These micro-organisms keep pathogens in check by creating an environment toxic for themselves and other micro-organisms by producing acid or alcohol. Do not ever be told that beer is not good for you…… Fermentation can also make foods more nutritious and palatable. For example, drinking water in the Middle Ages was dangerous because it often contained pathogens that could spread disease. When the water is made into beer, the boiling during the brewing process kills any bacteria in the water that could make people sick. Additionally, the water now has the nutrients from the barley and other ingredients, and the microorganisms can also produce vitamins as they ferment.

However, below I have listed the most practical survival methods of preserving your meat and fish.

CANNING
SEE https://www.youtube.com/watch?v=jU0CzxBnKoY

Canning involves cooking food, sealing it in sterilized cans or jars, and boiling the containers to kill or weaken any remaining bacteria as a form of sterilization. It was invented by the French confectioner Nicolas Appert. By 1806, this process was used by the French Navy to preserve meat, fruit, vegetables, and even milk. Although Appert had discovered a new way of preservation, it wasn't understood until 1864 when Louis Pasteur found the relationship between microorganisms, food spoilage, and illness.

Foods have varying degrees of natural protection against spoilage and may require that the final step occurs in a pressure cooker. High-acid fruits like strawberries require no preservatives to can and only a short boiling cycle, whereas marginal vegetables such as carrots require longer boiling and addition of other acidic elements. Low-acid foods, such as vegetables and meats, require pressure canning. Food preserved by canning or bottling is at immediate risk of spoilage once the can or bottle has been opened.

Lack of quality control in the canning process may allow the ingress of water or micro-organisms. Most such failures are rapidly detected as decomposition within the can cause gas production and the can will swell or burst.

Canning is very effective, but **do not be complacent in** your methods.... poor hygiene allowing contamination of canned food by the obligate anaerobe Clostridium botulinum, can produce an acute toxin within the food, leading to severe illness or death. This organism produces no gas or obvious taste and remains undetected by taste or smell. Its toxin is denatured by cooking, however. Cooked mushrooms, handled poorly and then canned, can support the growth of Staphylococcus aureus, which produces a toxin that is not destroyed by canning or subsequent reheating.

So in basic terms, canning is simply a way of preserving food through a process involving boiling the food inside glass jars and sealing the jars with lids. Where it can now often site for years in a safe edible manner and can even be eaten cold straight out of the jar.

If you are serious about stockpiling foods sufficient to last you and your family several months, then canning is the number one way to go without spending a fortune.

Even if you are not a serious gardener with a lovely big vegetable patch, it is still economical to buy your food in bulk whenever an item is on a special offer deal, take it home, and can it. There is the initial investment in glass jars and some equipment, but the savings and even the enjoyment in canning your own foods make it a hugely worthwhile investment.

For a home-based prepper, canning your own foods is a great way to go. The food tastes so superior to dried or salted food. Also, will not waste precious and maybe in short supply resource such as water.

There are many canning starter kits available on Amazon or E bay etc. These can be a really great way to begin, also look out for any local canning clubs or groups.... you may be very surprised at just how popular canning actually is. With an increase in awareness of the benefits of organic, vegan, and grow your own veg, etc. there is a revival in this traditional way to preserve and not waste such valued food.

Steps during canning
Different recipes will differ slightly on their specific instructions. However, all follow largely the same process: -
1. Carefully wash your fruit and veg. Remove any blemishes; look out for mold, black spots, or even bugs! Cut off any stems and the seed if required.
2. Blanch, boil, and prepare the food according to the recipe instructions. (blanching is an act of boiling fruit and veg for a few minutes, then placing in ice-cold water for a few minutes. This can help kill any enzymes and bacteria; it can also help loosed fruit skin should you want to remove it)
3. Using a ladle, fill your jars with liquid if this is part of the recipe.
4. Using a clean dishcloth, carefully wipe the rim of the glass jars.
5. Affix the lid and band on your glass jars.
6. Follow either the water bath or pressure cooker process, according to the recipe instructions.

Next stage, and without getting into too much fine detail, there are the two main methods of canning.

1. **WATER BATH canning method**
   Water bath canning is the process of using a large pot (bath) of boiling water to prepare your glass jars. In effect, you boil your submerged glass jars in boiling water for typically ten minutes. Note, vegetables and meat cannot use this process; they must use the "pressure cooker" canning process. This water bath method is more suited to canning fruits, jellies, jams, apple sauce, salsas, etc.

   This process is easily twice as fast as pressure cooker canning. Simply fill a large bath/pot with enough water to cover your ready filled glass jars. Ideally, use a canning rack to hold your jars inside the water bath/pot. Boil the water. Once it reached boiling temperature, most recipes will stipulate a 10-minute boil time.
   Once the 10 minutes are up, use a pair of jar tongs to remove the jars from the bath/pot. You may well hear a "popping" sound; this is quite

normal; it's the sound of the lids sealing down, which is what you want.

2. **PRESSURE COOKER canning method**
   The main difference comes down to the temperature generated. The pressure cooker traps in the steam produced from the boiled water. This steam increases the heat level dramatically in the pot. Water boils around 212 degrees Fahrenheit / 100 degrees Celsius, but this is not sufficient to fully kill the bacteria and enzymes found in meat and vegetables. However, the trapped steam generated using this method increases the temperature up to approx. 240 degrees Fahrenheit / 215 degrees Celsius, which is sufficient to make the food inside safe to eat in years to come.

Fill your pressure cooker with enough water to cover your tallest jar. Position the jars to close, but not actually touching. Lock the pressure cooker lid in place and attach the weighted pressure gauge. It may take about 10 minutes to reach the required pressure. Most recipes are processed at 10 psi, but always follow your recipe's instructions.

Once finished, use an oven-glove to trip the pressure cookers weighted gauge; this releases the pressure, it will be very, very hot. Once opened, remove the jars using jar tongs and allow to sit and cool off for 24 hours. Always check lids is sealed, to do this, press down on the centre of the lid; if the lid bounces up and down, then the seal failed. Either pop the failed jar in the fried ready for eating, or check your recipes as sometimes you can go through the pressure cooker process to try a second time to achieve a good seal. All that's left to do is to add a label with the jar contents and canning date. Always store somewhere cool, dark, and ventilated.

Search online or buy a book, hundreds of fabulous recipe ideas from jams and pickles to meats and veg

ROOT CELLARS
SEE
https://commonsensehome.com/root-cellars-101/#What_is_a_root_cellar

Pre modern-day refrigeration and freezers, an underground root cellar was an essential and commonplace way to store crops such as carrots, turnips, beets, parsnips, potatoes, and other root vegetables. Today, root cellars have made quite a comeback thanks to a revival in home vegetable and organic gardening. A root cellar will simply keep food from freezing during the winter and keep food cool during the summer to prevent spoilage.

A root cellar is a storage location that uses the natural cooling, insulating, and humidifying properties of mother earth. They are traditionally used by farmers and gardeners to store their raw vegetables.

To work effectively, a root cellar must hold a temperature of 32º to 40º Fahrenheit / 0° to 4.5°Celsius, with a humidity level of 85 to 95 percent.
The cool temperature slows the release of ethylene gas and stops the growth of microorganisms that cause the decomposition of the vegetables.
Whilst the high humidity level prevents loss of moisture through evaporation and the withering look that comes with it.

There are numerous guides online for the making of a Root cellar. I like the simple "Metal Dustbin" option or even multiple dustbins for storing different veg!

My personal favourite is The Dustbin root cellar (using a metal galvanised dustbin)
SEE https://www.youtube.com/watch?v=NedV9TPZCiQ

During winter, using a metal dustbin in a hole-in-the-ground cellar helps keep water out.
Dig a hole slightly larger than the diameter of the dustbin and deep enough so that the can's lid will sit 10cms / 4 inches above the soil level. Optional but also consider fitting a small ventilation pipe through the lid of the bin, hot air

rises and can thus escape, and cooler air falls. Also, drill a few holes in the base of the bin to allow any moisture build-up to escape. Add mesh screen over holes to keep out bugs, insects, and rodents. At this stage, I also like to add a 10cms / 4-inch layer of gravel below the bin; this is simply a safety measure to allow a fast soak away should rainwater enter the bins hole. Bear in mind that even during our worst of winters, it is usually only the first 30cms or foot down below ground affected, so any veg lower than a foot below the lid of the bin will be unaffected even during the coldest of nights. Heap soil around the circumference, add some straw inside the dustbin along with you veg, and cover the lid with straw and a sheet of plastic to keep everything fully watertight. Plus, you may even want to add an extra layer of insulation, something like your loft cavity insulation works really well.

Root vegetables will store perfectly well, even though the coldest of winters. You can use straw or sawdust and literally layer your vegetables one on top of the other. However, I find this difficult to inspect the produce, so I prefer using wooden trays designed to fit inside the dustbin, as it is far easier to remove these trays of veg and inspect them, and also rotate them. That said, you cannot store nearly as much veg as when layering, so there's a trade-off to consider.
Another popular option is to put a smaller bin inside the larger dustbin, with the same vent/base holes. This inner bin is far easier to remove to gain access to you veg and fruit stores.

If you are willing and able to construct a bigger purpose-built root cellar, here's are some key considerations to build into your plans: _
Complete temperature stability is only reached when you hit 3 metres / 10 feet depth.
Don't dig a root cellar near large trees; a tree's roots cannot only be difficult to dig through, but they will eventually grow and crack your cellar walls. (Although I've heard that putting a copper skin on the exterior of the walls will help, as apparently tree roots will avoid copper)
Inside, wooden shelving, bins, and platforms are the norm, as wood does not conduct heat and cold as rapidly as metal does.

Air circulation is critical for minimising airborne mold, so your wooden shelves should stand 3 to 8cms / 1 to 3 inches away from the walls.

For outdoor root cellars, packed earth is the preferred flooring. For purpose-built root cellars concrete floor work well and is practical for having your root cellar in a basement.

Every root cellar needs a thermometer and a hygrometer (to measure temperature and humidity, respectively), which should be checked every few days.

Heat is usually regulated using a ventilation pipe projecting up and outside. This allows cold air in, to help keep the temperature down.

TOP TIPS FOR STORING YOUR VEGETABLES

1. Stock your root cellar as late in the season as you can. If possible, chill the vegetables first in your fridge before putting them in your root cellar.
2. Some vegetables—such as potatoes, winter squash, garlic, pumpkins, and onions—need to be "cured" for a few days in a warm temperature before going into storage.
3. Shake off loose dirt rather than washing it off. Many root-cellar vegetables store far better this way, and leaving them wet will simply encourage them to rot. Carrots and beetroots are especially easy to store: just brush off any loose dirt, cut leaves back to about a 2cms / an inch above the root, and store roots in boxes of moist sand or peat moss.
4. Always handle your vegetables with great care; even slightly rough treatment can cause invisible bruising, which starts the produce on the road to decomposition.
5. Store cabbages and turnips in a separate root cellar, or a metal dustbin (see above) so their odour, which can be rather strong, will not permeate your other vegetables.
6. Think about where you place your vegetables: The driest and warmest air is near the ceiling; more-humid air is lower down. Most fruit "breathes," and some, for instance, apples and pear, should be wrapped in tissue paper or even old newspaper, to slow the release of ethylene gas, which can cause vegetables to spoil.

7. Vegetables stacked together to generate heat; this can lead to spoilage. Space out your vegetables on wooden shelves close to the floor and rotate the shelves every now and again. TIP: Wood shelving is naturally antibacterial. Wood also conducts heat more slowly than metal and doesn't rust. Avoid using treated woods.
8. Check your vegetables weekly, immediately removing any with early signs of rot or mold. Always remember the common verse, "One rotten apple spoils the whole barrel."

SALTING

This is a very old traditional process, favoured by the Royal Navy whose crew often lived on salted meats, which could sustain them during their long voyages. More practical at sea because you can simply boil seawater for your salt source, not so easy in the forest.

Salting is used because most bacteria, fungi, and other potentially pathogenic organisms cannot survive in a highly salty environment; this is due to the hypertonic nature of salt. Any living cell in such an environment will become dehydrated through osmosis and die or at least become temporarily inactivated.

Heavily rub in the salt, then air dry or smoke the flesh. The salt simply speeds up the whole drying out process. Before eating, wipe away excess salt or ideally wash it in clean water before eating.

SMOKING

Smoking will preserve meat and fish by both drying it out but also by creating a protective anti-microbial layer all over the flesh.

Using some embers from your main campfire, add in some green twigs (if dry, I suggest soaking them in water first). TIP. Do not let the embers get too hot; the idea is to "smoke" the flesh not actually cook it.

It's a slow process, keep feeding the embers with a mix of dry twigs and green twigs in order to both keep the fire alight and the smoke being produced. This can take about 24 hours to complete the process. You will know when it is done because as you bend the flesh, it will crack.

AIR-DRYING
If the weather is nice and the sun is shining, then this is a simple and good option for preserving small (squirrel sized) animals and fish.
1. Bleed, Gut and skin the animal (or fish).
2. Hang the carcass of the animals on a tree branch in direct sunlight and in a position with good airflow and breeze.
When the exterior looks completely dry, smooth, and break the carcass with a stone to expose its interior, bones, and marrow, then rehang for further drying.
3. Now cut the flesh into very small strips approx. 3cms long and just half a centimetre wide, trimming off as much fat as possible.
4. Hang these strips over a thin branch, but leave a space between them for better drying.
5. Leave it in place for approx. 24 hours until the meat is dry enough to snap (watch out for flies! You may well need to construct a cover or box to protect the food if flies are an issue)

PEMMICAN: The Ultimate Survival Food
During the Second Boer War, soldiers had to march for thirty-six hours on nothing but 4oz of pemmican and 4oz chocolate/sugar. All kept in a small iron tin- this is where the term "iron Rations" originated!

SEE
https://www.youtube.com/watch?v=MElMJsIP1Y0
https://www.youtube.com/watch?v=SJ9OjrnlH9g

Pemmican is a mixture of tallow, dried meat, and dried berries used as a nutritious food. Historically, it was an important part of indigenous cuisine in certain parts of North America and was a staple diet for Arctic explorers. The word comes from the Cree word pimîhkân, which itself is derived from the word pimî, "fat, grease".

Wild Food Foraging and Identification of poisonous plants
If you are in a wilderness survival situation, plants can, if chosen correctly, literally save life. There are two types of plants, "Edibles" or in Bear Grylls fab phrase, "Deadibles". I think this sums up the importance of choosing wisely pretty well.

My favourite book for wild food foraging is WILD FOOD UK: Marlow Renton and Eric Biggane "Foraging Pocket Guide" ISBN 978-1-9999222-2-1

There is a simple 6 step to use when trying to decide if a plant is edible or deadible...
1. **LOOK AT IT**
    Avoid bright coloured plants often, which can be nature's way of saying do not eat me. Does it look old or wilted, if it looks unappealing, it is best to avoid it.

2. **SMELL IT**
   Obvious smells to avoid are almonds or pears, as this can indicate poison and the presence of hydrocyanic acid. Also, does it smell "off" or rancid, another sign it is best avoided?
3. **SKIN RUB TEST**
   Crush a part of the plant you think might be safe to eat, then rub some of its liquid juice on your wrist. Then leave it a couple of hours and check if you develop any allergic reactions, even minor signs such as sore or redness. If no reaction, move to step 4.
4. **LIPS RUB TEST**
   The next stage is to rub some of the plant's juice on the very sensitive inside of your lips. If you get any tingling or any swelling, then thoroughly wash your mouth immediately.
5. **CHEW TEST**
   Chew a small piece and spit it out (do NOT swallow it at this stage) any tingling or any swelling, then thoroughly wash your mouth immediately.
6. **SMALL PORTION SWALLOW TEST**
   If all good so far, the final test is to eat a small amount. Then wait 4-6 hours and see what happens. During this time, do NOT drink or eat anything else, as all this will do is dilute the plant's effect and could give you false confidence that the plant is actually OK to be eaten.
   If all seems good and no adverse reactions, you are fairly safe to try eating a bigger portion, then after another 4-6 hours, know that it is safe to eat more!

Some surprising plants that are totally safe to eat include: -
Stinging Nettles: -

Once cooked, it kills the "sting" and these are actually quite nutritious. They can even be eaten raw. The trick to avoiding the "sting" is to pick it, squeeze it hard, pop it straight in your mouth and eat it quickly.
https://www.youtube.com/watch?v=ANZ60K3h2ow

Dandelions: -

An iconic looking plant is very easy to recognise. Kids love to blow the seeds of a bloomed dandelion. Best boiled to avoid its bitter taste. Everything, from the bright yellow flower down to the roots, is edible.
https://www.youtube.com/watch?v=-kfjULPC9jU

Oaktree, Acorn nuts: -

Acorns represent one of the biggest and most widespread calories in the wild plant food harvest, assuming you can beat the squirrels to them, at 2,000 calories per pound. Most acorns mature in late summer and begin falling from the trees in September or October. Do NOT try to eat green acorns; wait for the ripe brown ones!

Cooking Acorns: -Break them out of their shells, then soak in water for a few hours first as raw acorns contain tannin acid which can be toxic to humans and cause an unpleasant bitter taste. The easiest method is to lay out 20-30 acorns on a hard flat surface and smash them all at once with a rock. Now, remove all the shell fragments and place the nut pieces in a pot of water for a couple of hours (ideally use warm water to speed up the process). Do a taste test. If the acorns are still too bitter, soak them in warm water for another couple of hours.

Once dried, they can be ground into flour. This acorn flour can be used to bake bread; if you want soft spongy bread, mix in some wheat flour for its gluten. But If you don't mind the acorn's natural crumbly texture, use the acorn flour on its own. To roast them, add a sprinkle of salt and cook in a dry frying pan over your campfire. You can tell they're done when the colour has changed, and the nut pieces' smell like roasted nuts. Eat them just like you would peanuts.

Coffee substitute too, but don't expect caffeine, as there's no caffeine in an acorn, but you can roast a coffee substitute from acorns that is pleasant enough to drink. Place chunks of leached acorn in your pan and dry roast them. The roasting time will depend on the moisture in the nut pieces (more moist acorns need more time). Go with your eyes and nose when making acorn coffee, and stay right next to the pan. When the pieces are dark brown and give off a roasted (but not a burned) smell, they are ready. Add one tablespoon of the roasted acorn to one your cup of boiling water, leave for 5-10 minutes, reheat if necessary. Drink it "black" or with your usual milk and sugar.

Acorn Nutrition (1 oz.)
110 calories
7 grams of fat
12 grams carbohydrates
1.7 grams of protein

Acorn Medicine: - Save the brown tea-like water from when you first soaked the acorns. Crushed acorns in hot water can provide a great remedy for inflamed and irritated skin and toothache pains. Or you can make a liquid that's even more concentrated by boiling crushed acorns (leave in the crushed shells too) in a pint of water. Soak a clean cloth in the dark brown water, and apply this wet cloth to rashes, in-grown toenails, even haemorrhoid's. Leave the cloth in place, and repeat this treatment as often as needed. For toothache, simply wash the bitter water in your mouth like a mouth wash, but do not swallow, as the acidic water will give you a very upset stomach.
https://www.youtube.com/watch?v=wI7Gt21jn9A

Essential Rope Knots
In any survival situation, or even just in helping to build your shelter, knowing even a handful of essential knots will help make life so much easier.
The key with knots is to practice, practise and practise until tying them becomes a case of instinctive muscle memory!

I highly recommend buying this great little Knots Pocket Guide, with all the key knots you will ever need (COLLINS GEM "Knots" ISBN 978-0-00-719010-2)

OVERHAND KNOT
The simple fundamental knot almost all of us instinctively use. The overhand knot is a stopper, especially when used alone, and hence it is very secure, to the point of jamming badly. It should be used if the knot is intended to be permanent. It is often used to prevent the end of a rope from unravelling.

BOWLINE
The bowline, or more commonly one of its variations such as the double bowline, is sometimes used by climbers to tie the end of the rope to a climbing harness, or the like. The advantage of the bowline in this application is that the knot is easy to untie even after it has been loaded.
This knot makes a loop at the end of a rope which will not slip or tighten and can be very quickly tied. Often used to make a lifeline around a person waist and one of the reasons firefighters still use it today. It can even be tied one-handed, great if your other hands on the ladder!
"The rabbit comes out of the hole, goes around the tree and back down the hole."

CLOVE HITCH
The real advantage of a clove hitch is that you can quickly tie it in the middle of a rope. A simple knot for tying one end of a rope to a vertical pole or tree.

HIGHWAYMAN'S HITCH
The Highwayman's hitch is a quick-release draw hitch used for temporarily securing a load that will need to be released easily and cleanly. The hitch can be untied with a tug of the working end, even when under tension. Historically highwaymen used this knot to secure their horses as it can be very quickly released.

INTRODUCTION TO ADVANCED WATER COLLECTION TECHNIQUES
In wilderness survival situations, water is life and must be your main priority.
WARNING: Contaminated and non-filtered/purified water can not only make you very ill, but it can cause you to excrete far more water than you drank in the first place!

Always remember the basic survival rules and set your priorities accordingly: -
You can survive **three minutes** without breathable **air** (unconsciousness generally occurs), or in icy water.
You can survive **three hours** in a **harsh environment**, such as extreme heat or cold.
You can survive **three days** without drinkable **water**.
You can survive **three weeks** without **food**.

RIVERS/STREAMS
Although as an obvious choice, there are some basic precautions still to take:
1. Always collect water from fast-flowing areas rather than still or slow-moving parts. Ideally, water which is moving over rocks as this tends to be clean and debris free
2. A useful tip is to turn the neck of your water bottle downstream (i.e., Not facing the flow of the water). This technique helps avoid you collecting anything floating on the surface)

DRY RIVER BED
Quite often, if you dig down, there is often sub-surface water just below the dry river bed surface. Water should slowly seep in and fill it up. Again, boil or purify before drinking.

GYPSY WATER WELL
Also known as an Indian well, this is quite a clever little trick. When you find a dirty stagnant pool of water, simply dig a square approx. 50cms deep; positioned 30cms away from the pool. The water will slowly filter through the soil, which is between the 2 holes. Whilst not drinkable, it will definitely be far cleaner. Then boil or purify before drinking. Often best left overnight.

TIP: Position an angled stick firmly in the ground so any rodents or bugs that fall in, have a way to climb out.

ABOVE-GROUND SOLAR WATER STILLS
This is a popular survival trip. Because green leaves photosynthesize, they produce oxygen and also water vapour. All you need to do to collect this water vapour is to tie a plastic bag around a tree branch (Avoid poisonous trees/plants). Each bag will produce about an inch of water after several hours. So to be efficient, you need to tie several plastic bags in order to gather a reasonable amount of water!

BELOW GROUNDWATER STILLS
Another desert survival favourite this one. Dig a hole about 60cms deep and about 100cms diameter in a conical shape. At the bottom of the hole, put in a container to collect the water. Then cover the hole with a plastic sheet, help down by soil or rocks. Above your container, pierce a small hole so water can drip through, weight it down with a clean pebble.
WEIRD TIP: If you urinate in the hole before putting in your container, the water moisture part of your urine will condense onto the underside of the plastic sheet and drip into your container as clean water!

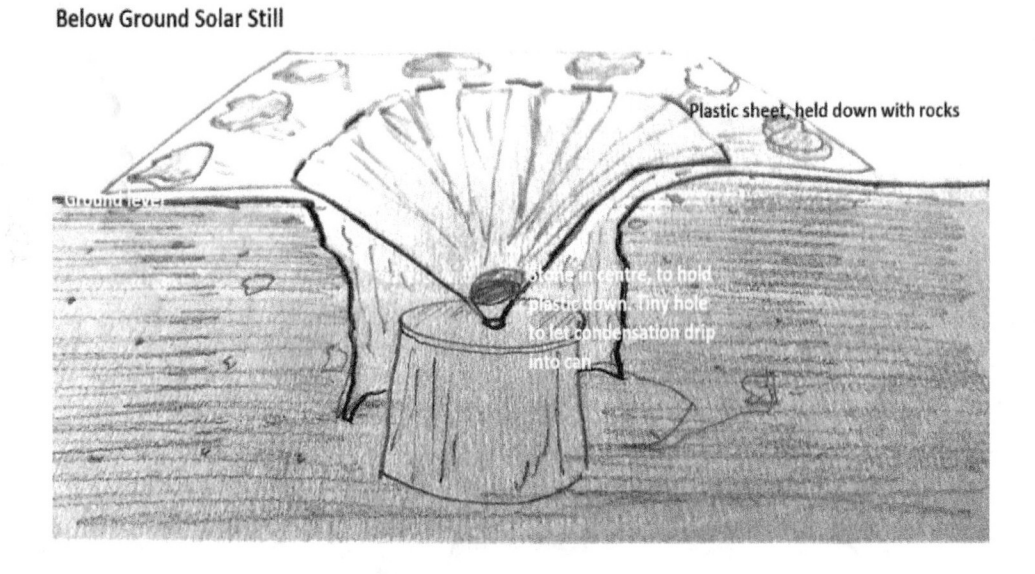

Below Ground Solar Still

DEW and MOSS WATER COLLECTION

Early morning time, you will often see a moisture dew on grass, leaves and vegetation. The easiest way to collect this is to tie a clean t-shirt or towel etc. around your lower legs and go for a walk rubbing against the plants. Once the material is saturated, wring it out and repeat.

If you spot any moss, this tends to act like a sponge, so give it a squeeze and more easy water collection.

FILTERING WATER

It is always worth carrying in your kit a water filtration method such as a water filtration straw. This device is used when you literally drink untreated water like using a normal straw. Inside the device is a filtration system that instantly makes the water safe to drink. Failing that water purification tables are great to also carry.

In a worse case, use your socks, or partner's tights (almost any fabric will work), add in some sand, and fine gravel-like rocks. Layer starting with the small and finest at the bottom and gradually getting bigger as you go higher…. Pour in the dirty water at the top, and by the time it filters through all the layers, it is pretty clean. Ideally, you should boil it before drinking, but in a survival situation, it will probably be fairly safe to drink without further treatment unless the water came from a very stagnant and dirty pool.

PURIFYING WATER

As mentioned above, always have a stash of water purification tablets with you, best kept in a waterproof plastic pouch for extra protection. They are typically chlorine, chlorine dioxide or iodine and these chemicals destroy bacteria, viruses and parasitic protozoans and leave the water safe to drink. Water purification tablets will make water safe to drink but will not remove debris or sediment, so filter the water first (methods as mentioned above) Add one tablet into the water, or if really disgusting water, maybe 2 or 3 will be needed. Leave for at least half an hour, the treated water may not taste great, but it will be safe to drink. The chlorine taste can be lessened by allowing the treated water to sit uncovered so the chlorine can evaporate.
WARNING: Iodine tablets may pose health risks for people with thyroid conditions or iodine allergies, or for women who are pregnant.

DRINKING YOUR OWN URINE: Last resort!
A process made famous by my TV hero Bear Grylls...

A healthy person's urine is about 95 percent water and sterile, so in the short term, it's safe to drink and does replenish lost water. The lighter the colour, the better, it is too dark and pungent, do not drink it; you're more likely to get ill instead of hydrated from it.

CHAPTER 10

STEP 7: Get trained in Krav Maga or similar Self Defence

Technique chosen by The Israeli Secret Service and Military, and believe me those guys and gals don't mess around.

Image courtesy of www.kravmaga-midlands.com
(I'm the one slightly to left of centre)

This form of "real life" self-defence training will be able to teach you all key essential basic techniques, enabling you to be better able to defend your loved ones, your property, and your preps. It will teach you the benefits of "Situational awareness," looking at signs and situations that are unfolding around you. This can often help you avoid violence from even starting! But if violence comes, it will equip you with a full complement of counter-attacking and brutal pre-emptive tactics to cover most eventualities. This is real-world training!

Most clubs will add in optional reality-based scenarios, kitting you out with safety gear such as helmets and pads! The purpose of this is for you to get realistic with the reality of being attacked with individuals or gang's intent on taking your stuff. Either from groups or individuals with anything from a baseball bat to a knife.

You will get to experience the sheer adrenaline, the fight or flight reflex, and the terror of such encounters…. but whilst in a safe and controlled environment whilst wearing the necessary safety gear to ensure your safety…. Give it your all, you may get some knocks and bumps, but this will be nothing compared to real-life events outside of the training centre and without the protection of safety helmets, pads, etc.

Key knowledge includes: -
- **Recognise potential conflict signs BEFORE you actually get attacked.**
  Situational awareness and understanding warning signs such as an aggressor having: -
  Red Face (getting angry) or worse colour drained from their face (Often a sign an attack is imminent)
  Prolonged eye contact
  Raised voice and gritted teeth
  Faster breathing, almost panting whilst talking
  Clenching and unclenching fists
  Shoulders tensing and head dropping
  Stance moving from square one, to sideways fighting stance
  Hands raised to above waist position (enable far better defences from attack, and or, faster attack)
- **Run away if you can**
  This can be problematic if you are with friends/family, or if you are wearing your "Bug Out" rucksac
- You will never win a defensive fight trying simply to protect yourself. Strike first and strike fast and don't stop until you know your attacker can no longer attack you. Real-life fights are not pretty, but you must win, whatever the cost

- **Targets their weak points**
  Eyes, throat, groin
- **Train and practise**
  Your pre-emptive attacks and your defences must be explosively delivered and need to be so well practised that they are instinctive muscle memory...You will not have time to think and plan in most real-life fights!

An introduction to a few key techniques and a list of main areas to train in
• General threat assessment and awareness to potential dangers. Body positioning and punching technique
• Basic blocks and counter-attacks
• How to escape from chokes/holds/grabs etc.
• Ground fighting
• Knife and stick (baseball bat) defences
• Mock attacks / defensive training. Ideally involving 2 or 3 attacker scenarios.

For example of training videos, please take a look at
https://bz-online-videos.com/free-vod/

CHAPTER 11

Conclusion, summary, and further advancement

Prepping is a journey, a lifestyle, and ultimately, it becomes a hobby. It also requires constant learning and acquisition of new skills and techniques You may want to consider starting a family, friends, and neighbour's prepper group. Shared supplies and skillsets. Also, more hands to cover better defences against looters etc.

Key core skills needed to further develop your own knowledge of: -
- Navigation and Map Reading
- Extreme trauma first aid skills
- Natural Medical remedies
- Building an outdoor compost toilet
- Water harvesting and advanced filtration methods
- Further Wild food foraging
- Advanced Snares/Trapping for wild animals such as rabbits and squirrels
- Wild game butchery skills
- Advanced shelter building
- Bread Making over a campfire
- Advanced home canning, pickles, jams, etc.
- Building a Faraday cage to protect your electronics from an EMP strike
  The simplest option is to buy a galvanised metal dustbin, one with a tight-fitting lid.

CHAPTER 12

Index

Index 1

Knife Law In The Uk

Selling, buying, and carrying knives
Please contact your local police to check if a knife or weapon is illegal when in doubt.
Info courtesy of https://www.gov.uk/buying-carrying-knives

Surprising to most people, even telescopic truncheons - extend automatically by pressing a button or spring in the handle are illegal to carry; as are Knuckledusters!

SELLING, BUYING, AND CARRYING KNIVES IN UK
The maximum penalty for an adult carrying a knife is 4 years in prison and an unlimited fine.
You'll get a prison sentence if you're convicted of carrying a knife more than once.
Basic UK laws on knives
It's illegal to:
Sell a knife to anyone under 18, unless it has a folding blade 3 inches long (7.62 cm) or less

153

Carry a knife in public without good reason, unless it has a folding blade with a cutting edge 3 inches long or less
Carry, buy or sell any type of banned knife
Use any knife in a threatening way (even a legal knife)
Scotland
In Scotland, 16 to 18-year-olds are allowed to buy cutlery and kitchen knives.
Lock knives
Lock knives are not classed as folding knives and are illegal to carry in public without good reason.
Lock knives have blades that can be locked and refolded only by pressing a button
This can include multi-tool knives - tools that also contain other devices such as a screwdriver or can opener

Banned knives and weapons

It is illegal to bring into the UK, sell, hire, lend, or give anyone the following.
Disclaimer: *this list is not exhaustive, and it is your responsibility to check current laws*
Butterfly knives (also known as 'balisongs') - a blade hidden inside a handle that splits in the middle
Disguised knives - a blade or sharp point hidden inside what looks like everyday objects such as a buckle, phone, brush, or lipstick
Flick knives (also known as 'switchblades' or 'automatic knives') - a blade hidden inside a handle which shoots out when a button is pressed
Gravity knives
Stealth knives - a knife or spike not made from metal (except when used at home, for food or a toy)
Zombie knives - a knife with a cutting edge, a serrated edge, and images or words suggesting it is used for violence
Swords, including samurai swords - a curved blade over 50cm (with some exceptions, such as antiques and swords made to traditional methods before 1954)
Sword-sticks - a hollow walking stick or cane containing a blade
Push daggers
Blowpipes ('blow gun')

Telescopic truncheons: extend automatically by pressing a button or spring in the handle
Batons: straight, side-handled, or friction-lock truncheons
Hollow kubotans: a cylinder-shaped keychain holding spikes
Shurikens (also known as 'shaken', 'death stars' or 'throwing stars')
Kusari-gama: a sickle attached to a rope, cord, or wire
Kyoketsu-shoge: a hook-knife attached to a rope, cord, or wire
Kusari (or 'manrikigusari'): a weight attached to a rope, cord, wire
Hand or foot-claws
Knuckledusters

Good reasons for carrying a knife or weapon
Examples of good reasons to carry a knife or weapon in public can include:
Taking knives you use at work, to and from work
Taking it to a gallery or museum to be exhibited
If it'll be used for theatre, film, television, historical re-enactment or religious purposes, for example, the kirpan some Sikhs carry
If it'll be used in a demonstration or to teach someone how to use it

REMEMBER: a court will decide if you've got a good reason to carry a knife or a weapon if you're going to be charged with carrying it illegally.

Index 2

Bibliography of books I have enjoyed and found useful. Definitely worth a read

Below are some of my key "Prepper" or "Living Off Grid" type books

Most of these inspired me to some extent in writing this "Prepper" book.

1. Bear Grylls "How To Stay Alive"   ISBN 978-0-552-16879-3
   Our own UK and much loved survival expert. Bear must be a prepper...he even owns his own private island off the Welsh coast.

2. Mike Robinson "Fit For Table"   ISBN 978-1-84689-006-2
   I also attended The Mike Robinson "Game and Wild Food Cookery School" in Berkshire, UK, back in 2014
   An informative, hands-on and very enjoyable days' course

3. David George "UK Prepping"   ISBN 9781976991394
   Pamphlet style book, bit dark but some good ideas and worst case scenarios info

4. Bill Cobb "Canning For Preppers"   ISBN 9781505365078
   Small pamphlet guide, but with some good info

5. Daisy Luther "The Preppers Water Survival Guide"
   ISBN 9781612434483

6. Dave Canterbury "The Bushcraft Field Guide"
   ISBN 13-978-1-4405-9852-4

7. J.D. Rockefeller "Your Preppers Supplies Guide"
   ISBN 9781539760412
   Small pamphlet style book, but with some good info

8. Jim Cobb "Countdown To Prepardness"   ISBN 978-1-61243-304-2

9. Jim Cobb "Preppers Long-Term Survival Guide"
   ISBN 9781612432731

10. Michel Daniek "DIY 12V Solar Power"
    ISBN 978-1-85623-242-5

11. Nina Stere "Prepper Handbook"   ISBN 9781519798008
    A small pamphlet book, with some good info

12. Novato Press "Prepper Supplies and Survival Guide"
    ISBN 978-1-62315-258-1

13. Rockridge Press "The Preppers Cookbook"
    ISBN 978-1-62315-197-3

14. Scott Hunt "Complete Guide To Disaster Preparedness"
    ISBN 978-1-250-05564-4

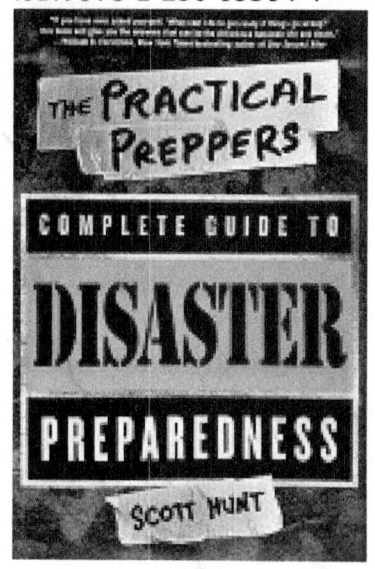

15. Timothy S. Morris "Preppers Survival Medicine Handbook" ISBN 9781505233100
    Pamphlet type book, but with lots of great info

16. WILD FOOD UK: Marlow Renton and Eric Biggane "Foraging Pocket Guide" ISBN 978-1-9999222-2-1
    Cannot recommend this book enough.

17. COLLINS GEM "Food For Free" ISBN 978-0-00-718303-6
    Fantastic Pocket Guide, with lots of great info

18. COLLINS GEM "Knots" ISBN 978-0-00-719010-2
    Fantastic Pocket Guide, with all the key knots you will ever need

19. COLLINS GEM "Mushrooms" ISBN 978-0-00-718307-4
    Fantastic Pocket Guide on safe foraging for mushrooms

20. Angler Vardamir "SURVIVAL HACKS" ISBN 9798679238275
    Some useful if quirky hacks, ideas, and survival tips in this book

21. THE TRAPPERS BIBLE   ISBN 978 1 61608 559 9
    Big old school book on trapping and hunting.
    Really good vintage-styled book

22. COMPLETE KRAV MAGA   ISBN 978 1 56975 573 0
    Darren Leving / John Whitman

23. KRAV MAGA   ISBN 0 7499 2591 4
    David Kahn

Index 3

Acknowledgments and thanks

My thanks to all the authors, bloggers, and writers of everything bushcraft, prepping, and to do with survival. I salute you all and thank you for sharing your experience and knowledge.

Big thanks to David and his team at **Ink Digital** for designing this book cover, blog pages, and our new web site www.inkdigital.co.uk

Thanks to **Pixabay** for access to their copyright-free image library www.pixabay.com

Thanks also **Getty Images** for their paid-for range of images www.istockphoto.com

Thanks to **CORPORALS CORNER** for the use of his Log Rocket Stove photo, check out his Amazon shop, YouTube videos, and Facebook page.

Thanks to **Bartosz Zukowski** at www.kravmaga-midlands.com and all club members in the group photo I was part of. An awesome Krav Maga club full of friendly, dedicated people.

And also to **Al Natrins**, especially for his one-to-one Krav Maga training www.kravmayhem.com

Also, special thanks to my family and friends for their numerous proof-reading critiques of this book throughout the writing process. In particular, special thanks to my big sis **Debbie Dawson** for her extra efforts and for her advice with the medical side of things. *Much love* x

Printed in Great Britain
by Amazon